ROBERT NICHOLLS

SURVIVING THE DARKNESS

LESSONS LEARNED FROM
A BATTLE WITH DEPRESSION AND ANXIETY

First published 2020
Copyright © 2020. Robert Nicholls.
Robert Nicholls asserts his right to be known as the author of this book.
All rights reserved. No part of this book may be reproduced, stored in a retrieval system, communicated or transmitted in any form or by any means, electronic, mechanical, photocopying, recording or otherwise, without prior written permission of the publisher.

A catalogue record for this work is available from the National Library of Australia

ISBN 978-0-6488865-0-1 (paperback)
ISBN: 978-0-6488865-1-8 (ebook)
Cover and text design by Nada Backovic
Cover image: iStockphoto
Editing by The Expert Editor

Disclaimer

The information contained in this book provides general information only. It is not intended as, and should not be relied upon as, a substitute for advice and therapy by appropriately qualified and licensed health care providers. The reader should regularly consult a doctor, psychologist or other appropriate professionals in matters relating to his/her health and particularly concerning any symptoms that may require diagnosis, medical or psychiatric attention. To the maximum extent permitted by law, the author and publisher disclaim all responsibility and liability to any person, arising directly or indirectly from any person taking or not taking action based on the information in this publication.

This book is dedicated to people that have lost their lives through depression and anxiety, and to their families still trying to cope with the tragedy.

CONTENTS

Foreword	1
CHAPTER ONE: INTO THE DARKNESS	**5**
Doctor, I have a few questions	7
The shadow boxer	9
What caused me to be depressed?	13
How long will it last?	14
What treatments are available?	15
CHAPTER TWO: THE BLACK HOLE	**17**
The status quo	17
No fuel in the tank	19
Why is everything blue?	20
All pain, no pleasure	21
Why can't I concentrate?	22
Beware of the black dog!	23
I am a failure	24
Adjusting the belt	26
To sleep or not to sleep—that is not the question	26
Mountains from molehills	27
Enter anxiety	27
CHAPTER THREE: BARRIERS TO TREATMENT	**31**
Back to the railway station	31
Stigma	32
Perceptions become a reality	35
Symptoms as barriers	37
Adequacy of support	37
Lack of resources	38

CHAPTER FOUR: NO PAIN. NO GAIN. — 41
Medications — 41
Psychotherapies — 42
Exercise and lifestyle choices — 43
The keys to successful treatment — 43

CHAPTER FIVE: COPING STRATEGIES — 47
Coping strategies that worked — 48
Important lessons learned — 60
Other alternatives — 67

CHAPTER SIX: YOUR RECOVERY TEAM — 69
Selecting your therapist — 70
Who can be your therapist? — 70
How do I find a psychologist? — 71
What to consider when making the choice — 71
What to expect in your first few therapy sessions — 75
Identifying warning signs — 78
Finding a therapeutic alliance — 79
What is 'good' therapy? — 80
During the sessions — 82
After the sessions — 82
Evaluating other team members — 82

CHAPTER SEVEN: PRACTICAL TIPS FOR CARERS AND SUPPORTERS — 85
Platitudes do not cure depression — 86
Table 1: What not to say — 88
No magic words — 95
Table 2: What to say — 96
Warning signs — 109

A note about warning signs	113
Prevention tips	114
Self-care for the supporter	115
CHAPTER EIGHT: BEYOND DARKNESS	**117**
What did you think?	120
Acknowledgments	121
Endnotes	123
About the Author	154

FOREWORD

This is a practical book about coping with depression and paving the way to recovery. Its purpose is to assure those suffering from depression that there is hope. Not only hope but genuine pathways to recovery through self-discovery, change and personal growth. With appropriate treatment, personal commitment and assistance from family and friends (your Recovery Team), the key messages that you will take away from your reading will assist you on your journey.

I will share with you my passage through depression and anxiety, the symptoms I experienced, the issues I confronted and the coping mechanisms I used to curtail my often volatile relationship with these illnesses.

In the interests of making this book more practical, I have deliberately refrained from offering a complete memoir of all my personal experiences with depression and anxiety. In doing so, I focus less on personal anecdotes and more on the learning derived from my experiences. While I do provide, where relevant, a significant level of detail of my own encounters to highlight various points, I think this approach is preferred for several reasons.

By avoiding an unduly exhaustive description of specific events that I experienced, I have attempted to mitigate against the risk of making my personal episodes analogous to your own or, worse still, providing a trigger for your own symptoms or a barrier to your recovery pathways. This has been tempered by my desire to extrapolate my experiences in sufficient detail to provide you with the intended practical benefits of this book.

I have also elected to restrict the length of the book sufficiently to offer the essential components of practical guidance in a concise and informative way. People with depression often struggle to find the mood, energy and motivation to read (or do anything for that matter), so by making the book as succinct as possible, I have attempted to afford sufferers with an opportunity to gain the maximum amount of practical assistance in the shortest possible time.

To some extent, while the factual context is important, the intricacies of my story are superfluous because everybody that suffers from mental illness will experience it in their own unique way even though there will be shared aspects of the journey, such as some of the symptoms and obstacles that are typically encountered, which I outline. In this context, I consider it important for you to understand that you will experience your own version of the illness and hopefully benefit more from the things that I have learned than the detailed factual circumstances that gave rise to these lessons.

I will not sugar-coat anything. There is no practical benefit to you in doing so.

For those supporting someone with mental illness, I have devoted a chapter to providing practical guidance and tools to assist you in becoming the most active contributor of support that you can be in the circumstances.

I am also hopeful the information and experiences shared go some way towards dispelling the myths, stigma, and the unreasonable inferences that society still draws about people with mental health issues and related illnesses.

Information presented in this book may be confronting, and a trigger to some people. If you are having suicidal thoughts, contact your local suicide prevention hotline for support and assistance. If you or a loved one is in immediate danger, call the emergency services number in your area. Information on your local mental health resources is also likely to be accessible online.

Australian health promotion charity, CheckPoint, maintain a Global Mental Health Directory which includes local website and emergency contact information for anywhere in the world. You can find the directory at https://checkpointorg.com/global/.

Just remember, you are never alone.

CHAPTER ONE: INTO THE DARKNESS

*Look at how a single candle can both
defy and define the darkness.*
— ANNE FRANK

When I was nineteen years old, I was a sworn police officer in the New South Wales[1] Police Force. Early one morning in 1990, I went with other officers to Newtown[2] Railway Station as part of my duties. It was peak hour. A man in his early twenties had committed suicide. He had been suffering from depression.

Almost two years later, Daniel Pollock did the same thing, taking his own life in the same way, by walking in front of a train, at the same railway station. This time, I was not there. Daniel was an Australian actor playing the character of Davey in the 1992 Australian drama film *Romper Stomper,* starring alongside Russell Crowe. He was also in his early twenties. Daniel died before the release of the movie and was posthumously awarded Best Supporting Actor at the 1992 Australian Film Industry Awards. He was famous and had a bright future, but depression did not care. It did not discriminate.

These were the first times in my life that I had even heard the word 'depression'. I do not recall thinking any more about it for some time. When I did, it was twenty-five years later. I had no choice.

I was sitting in the waiting room of my doctor's surgery. I knew that something was not right. It had taken a lot of time and effort even to get there. I was always tired, extraordinarily lazy, and lacked the energy for even the most basic of everyday tasks. I could not focus, retain new information or recall detail that I had been proficient in eliciting only several weeks before. Concentrating on work was impossible. Even the rudimentary aspects of my work as a lawyer and business advisor became untenable.

I was not motivated and lost interest in hobbies, exercise, friends, family and all other aspects of my life. I could not explain why I always felt so deeply and profoundly sad, worthless, angry, and irritable all at the same time. Nor why, suddenly, I considered myself a failure and life to be hopeless. I felt guilty and remonstrated with myself persistently over past events or minor personal shortcomings, seemingly incapable of letting them go. I felt so alone, helpless, and not worthy of love or attention from anyone. I often cried and for no apparent reason. I just wanted to sleep. At least when I did, the pain of these unsolicited and uninvited new feelings would subside. I was starting to eat more. I drank alcohol to excess to try to ease the pain. It would not go away.

I had never felt this way before. Each day was the same, each one a struggle under mounting pressure fuelled by the way that I was feeling physically and mentally. I felt utterly lost, out of control and isolated from my own body and mind. I wanted to be left alone. I wanted to die.

It was late September 2016.

After a few more visits to the doctor and some tests, I discovered that I had depression. At the time of my diagnosis, I had just turned forty-seven. It was at this point that my journey with this illness began. The black dog[3] had bitten me. The bite marks would take a long time to heal.

Doctor, I have a few questions

After my initial diagnosis, I had a few unanswered questions.

> *How will I explain depression to my friends, colleagues, and family?*
> *What is causing me to be depressed?*
> *How long will it last?*
> *What treatments are available?*

These seem like logical questions, right? I thought so but finding the answers would turn out to be an intensive, time-consuming and (at times) frustrating process.

It does not take long to discover that there is a plethora of information available from an equally diverse array of sources. Often, these references are highly technical, overly scientific, and not practical. Most of it is written by scientific researchers, academics, and health care clinicians, each in the pursuit of advancing the body of knowledge in their respective fields of expertise.

In my work, I had been accustomed to reading and understanding complex issues and concepts. However, I quickly learned that it would take years to read and try to digest it all sufficiently to respond to my fundamental questions. If you have ever read academic research papers, you will understand my point. It was surprising to find that research and medical science did not have all the answers, particularly regarding the causes for depression,[4] frequency of misdiagnosis,[5] and practical strategies to adopt when seeking treatment and to respond to treatment barriers in a meaningful way.

That is not to say that these resources were not helpful. Quite the contrary—they were. It is just that searching for answers to these questions while you are still suffering is arduous. Compiling relevant information and deciphering the good from the bad (and sometimes, the ugly) is a chore. I will save you some of the pain here because I will refer to several information sources that I found useful. I discovered the most helpful resources were written by people that had suffered or were still suffering from depression themselves. Personal sufferers tended to be more direct, practical, and less fascinated by technical terminology, lists of symptoms and diagnostic tools or guidelines.

Most of the self-help books and other publications dealing with mental illness tend to focus on the well-documented and traditional forms of treatment and recovery. I will talk about these and other methods in Chapter Four. Depending on my progress or even how my day was going, I learned these methods were not always practical.

Also, a lot of writers in this area talk about 'steps' to recovery, akin to the types of recovery platforms known to addiction (drugs, alcohol, and gambling, as examples). Under these systems, you pass through one 'step' (or stage) before progressing to the next in the same way before completing the final step to recovery. My experience with depression is that it is better to refer to 'pathways' that you take rather than individual 'steps'. There are a couple of reasons for this.

First, there is no one initial step, or successive steps, that you must satisfy before you move onto the next within your system of recovery. Second, it is possible (and highly probable) that you will take different directions at varying stages of your illness without necessarily starting at one point or another. I liken recovery to a maze with several possible routes to the exit. You might try one, find that it is not for you and then select another. You might then decide that the first one you tried was the better of the two options. Ultimately your sole objective is to get to the end. There just might be many different pathways to arrive at the destination. You get to choose which route to try first and last. There is no order to it. Hence, no steps required.

You may be surprised to learn the best source of information about how to respond to most of these questions is not the articles, books, blogs, and posts at your disposal. The only person that knows what you are feeling and what recovery program will work best for you is YOU. All you need are the tools to make it happen. In responding to my illness over several years and continually seeking answers, I have discovered a range of tools and additional techniques that have assisted me in my battle with depression and anxiety. I will share these with you later in this book.

The shadow boxer

I think it is critical to have at least a basic understanding of the disease and its prevalence around the world. Without that context, it is easy to misunderstand it or, worse still, underestimate its potential impact. It is also important to highlight a vital message for you to keep in the back of your mind throughout your journey, particularly in the dark times.

Most people will have had some experience with depression and anxiety, whether it is personal or through their family, friends, or work colleagues. In 2017, more than two hundred and sixty-four million people of all ages were affected by depression,[6] equating to approximately 3.5 per cent of the global population.[7] In some countries,[8] the proportionate rate was higher than the world figure, highlighting to varying degrees the prevalence of depression in all societies around the globe.

Research suggests that the share of the population with depression ranges between 2 per cent and 6 per cent around the world today.[9] It has become a leading cause of disability worldwide and is a significant contributor to the overall global burden of disease.[10] This burden is on the rise globally.[11]

Here is the crucial message. Depression is common. A lot of people experience it and will continue to do so. That means that people with depression are not alone. They are never alone.

In the same way that people are unique, the severity and impact of depression are different in each case. Still, there are also some universal experiences that can be shared to benefit your recovery. It also follows that people before you have learned to survive and recover from the illness, and go on to lead healthy, productive, and happy lives. You can do that too.

Outside the well-documented symptoms, psychiatric criteria, and technical guidelines, very few people have conveyed what it is like to have depression. Some have tried. The 'black hole that there is no way to climb out of (nor point in doing so)'.[12] The black dog.[13] The 'darkness,'[14] which 'alienates you from your work, your passions, and the people around you. That, in turn, pulls you further into the darkness and allows it to do further damage. Things that once brought you joy – like "rainbows" and "views" – come to seem like they do not matter. You would previously have turned to them to restore your happiness, but they no longer have that effect. Hence, you wind up, stuck there, in the darkness.'[15]

In the beginning, one of the most challenging things is that it is not easy to explain to those around you what it is like to have depression, particularly those people that have never suffered or had experience with it. I still struggle to come to grips with some sort of explanation.

Depression is a remorselessly corrosive agent of the soul. It takes you to a dark, unpredictable, and morbid place that makes you question your existence almost every moment of nearly every day and, at times, pray for it to end. If you let it, it will destroy everything about you and your life. Before it does so, it tortures you, day by day, night by night, until you have nothing left but relentless pain and misery.

More than likely, depression will also make you feel like the worst person in the world. It can make you feel responsible for events and situations for which you are not even remotely responsible but feel compelled to assume a burden of guilt for them, nevertheless. The illness can make you feel sinister, dirty, and melancholy all at the same time. In your own mind, you become the bad guy, the villain, the archenemy of everything that is good. But depression is a liar, a cheat, and a thief. It deliberately misleads, steals everything from you and yields nothing in return but prolonged anguish.

Ultimately, the mission (should you choose to accept it) is to convince yourself that, like the performance of a magician, depression is a clever act of illusion designed to deceive and deprive your mind of the reality. Hope is the panacea to recovery but finding it while you are afflicted can be elusive. It can also be both challenging and confronting. To rediscover hope requires hard work, genuine self-discovery, a commitment to change and acceptance that you are unlikely to discover your pathways to recovery on your own and without support from your Recovery Team.

Battling this illness is like boxing at shadows. If you want out, you must keep swinging. Ultimately, you will land a punch. If you are to knock it out, you must give it your best shot.

Another way of arriving at some explanation is to relate depression to what it is not.

Depression is different from usual mood fluctuations and short-lived emotional responses to challenges in everyday life.[16] While everyone has felt sad, depression is different. It is essential to understand that depression is a mental condition. A lot of people confuse depression with sadness. One may be a symptom of the other, but it does not necessarily mean they are the same.[17]

Depression is unique and characterised by well recognised and documented life-cycle risk factors,[18] symptoms,[19] types[20] and diagnostic guidelines.[21] Symptoms are prevalent nearly every day, persist for extended periods and result in a significant change in a person's 'normal' mood.[22] Depressive disorders occur with varying severity,[23] ranging from mild to moderate (or persistent depression, dysthymia) to severe (or major depressive disorder).[24]

An individual with a mild depressive episode is usually distressed by the symptoms and has some difficulty in continuing with everyday work and social activities but will probably not cease to function altogether.[25] During a severe depressive episode, it is improbable that the sufferer will be able to continue with social, work, or domestic activities, except to a minimal extent.

Periods of low mood or difficulty are typical for humans, however, these feelings usually pass for most people.[26] The difference between a low mood and depression is observed when an individual's feelings consistently interfere with their daily life over a minimum period of two weeks.[27]

The severity and duration of depressive episodes that lead to depression overtaking your life and becoming your life's focus[28] distinguishes it from the everyday low mood, which may conversely come and go periodically without any substantive impact on your day-to-day life. The other notable point of distinction is that, with depression, thoughts of death (as opposed to dying, which we all think about from time to time) are pervasive. They remain with you throughout your journey with the illness.

What caused me to be depressed?

You should not expect a complete answer to this question from academic research or medical science. While you may never know the exact cause of your depression, it is highly likely that you will at least be introduced to some possibilities at various stages of your treatment, whether from therapy, self-help, or other remedy options.

Depression is a complex condition. Its causes are not fully understood,[29] remain mostly unknown,[30] and vary according to individual circumstances.[31] Research suggests that depression may result from a complex interaction of social, psychological, environmental, and biological factors [32] (including genetics).[33] These factors influence the prevalence[34] of depression, evidencing the existence of some common trends among countries globally.[35]

Although the exact reasons why depression manifests are unclear,[36] risk factors are well-known.[37] For example, people who have gone through adverse life events (unemployment, bereavement, psychological trauma) are more likely to develop depression.[38]

While the reasons for people experiencing depression and its incidence vary, it does not discriminate.[39] It does not matter how old you are.[40] A woman or a man.[41] Married or single. An adult or a child.[42] Nor does it care where you live,[43] what you do for work, where you went to school, college or university,[44] where you come from,[45] or whether you are rich, poor, famous or infamous (or a combination of these).[46]

It follows that we should not be at all surprised that depression will make an appearance in our lives, or the life of someone we know, at some time during our existence on the planet.

We are all vulnerable.

How long will it last?

If you broke your arm, a doctor could advise how many weeks you were likely to need a cast before recovering from this type of injury. Unfortunately, depression is not like that.

Episodes of depression can vary in duration from weeks to years but typically last for a minimum of several weeks.[47] For some people, depression is a long-term illness.

The duration of the illness depends on your diagnosis. Your diagnosis stems from the duration and severity of your symptoms, any responses to treatment or recurring risk factors.[48]

Depression is often chronic and recurrent.[49] One study found that fewer than one-third of patients recovered and remained well in the eighteen months after an episode of depression.[50] According to the American Psychiatric Association,[51] at least 50 per cent of people who have experienced an episode of major depression will go on to have a second. About 80 per cent of people who have two events will have a third. These figures highlight the importance of treatment and the need for it to focus on maintaining wellness and preventing relapse.[52]

The simple, practical answer is that it lasts until you recover. Getting the right treatment is vital. I will talk about treatment options and coping strategies later in the book.

What treatments are available?

Untreated, depression can cause the affected person to suffer greatly and function poorly at work, at school, college or university, and in the family.[53]

At its worst, depression can lead to suicide, which has a devastating impact on families, friends, and whole communities.[54] Globally, close to eight hundred thousand people die due to suicide each year, which is about one person every forty seconds.[55] According to research, depression plays a role in more than one-half of all suicide attempts,[56] and individuals with depression are twenty times more likely to die from suicide than someone without it.[57] Importantly, this does not mean that most people with depression will suicide or attempt it.[58] Most will not do so.

In Chapter Three, I talk about some barriers you are likely to experience before and during your treatment. This information will get you prepared to confront some common obstacles and avoid the negative impact these can have on your active treatment. In Chapter Four, I outline standard treatment options and provide some practical assistance, based on my experience, to assist you with the development of your recovery plan.

One critical message in this context is that it is possible to recover from depression and, regardless of the treatment options, the most effective recovery will also be directed by you[59] because the pathway chosen by you is always the right one.

ROBERT NICHOLLS

CHAPTER TWO: THE BLACK HOLE

I always believe if you're stuck in a hole and maybe things aren't going well, you will come out stronger. Everything in life is this way.

— ROGER FEDERER

The status quo

At the time of my diagnosis, I was working as a specialist business lawyer, accredited mediator, and business consultant in Australia. In 2011, I had started my practice, and it had grown significantly. In monetary terms, I was successful. More importantly, I was happily married (since 1996) and a proud dad to two great kids (young adults). My family was safe, prosperous, and healthy.

Like most small-business owners, I worked long hours under conditions of high stress and intensity. That was the nature of the work and operating a growing professional services business. It was not unusual to work seven days per week, seventy to eighty hours per week. A lot of lawyers and business owners do that. Holidays were rare. Time off was a novelty.

Before I became a lawyer in 1997, I graduated with a law degree from the University of Technology, Sydney, while working full-time as a police prosecutor in the New South Wales Police Force and part-time on weekends in my wife's bistro. I later obtained my Master of Business degree and other postgraduate qualifications, also while working and, by that time, raising a young family.

For twenty-five years or so, I moved in and out of legal and management roles. In 2008, I worked as the Managing Director and CEO of a public company listed on the Australian Stock Exchange. At the end of that contract, I started my legal and business consulting practice. Almost six years later, I had depression and anxiety. My life (and the lives of my immediate family) changed forever.

According to my friends and family, I was hardworking, a perfectionist, fiercely loyal and dedicated to protecting those around me. A rock to my family and friends. A sounding board to those who needed someone to talk to and someone who would do anything to help a friend or family member in need. I was compassionate, articulate, confident, optimistic and had a good sense of humour. To my colleagues, I was professional, competent, an effective leader, a valuable team member and, when it came to it, a tough adversary.

I also changed. Ultimately, I became a different, better person.

I have given you some background about me to illustrate a couple of points. First, I was just an ordinary guy working hard to support his family and to build a legacy from my intellect and labour. I was a business owner. I was no different to billions of other people doing the same thing, regardless of their job title, trade, or profession. Second, it highlights the point made in the first chapter. Depression does not give one iota about your level of education, how much money you have or the work you do. No one is immune from the vulnerability of risk factors or a diagnosis of depression. Last, ignoring the risk factors (like extended periods of sustained stress and a lack of balance between work and leisure time)[60] is not a smart thing to do. It is like playing with fire. You are always running the risk of getting burnt.

According to the National Institute of Mental Health,[61] not everyone who is depressed experiences every symptom. While there are a number of common signs and symptoms,[62] some people experience only a few symptoms, while others may experience many.[63] The severity and frequency of symptoms and how long they last will vary depending on the individual and type of depressive episode. Symptoms may also vary depending on the stage of the illness.[64]

A key message in this chapter is that depression affects everyone differently at various stages of the illness. Symptoms and their effects are a 'normal' part of having depression. There are, however, ways of dealing with them, which we will explore in later chapters.

I will now talk about some of the signs and symptoms that I experienced at various stages and with different levels of intensity during my illness. In practical terms, a lot of symptoms overlap and interact with each other. Your symptoms may vary. You may experience one with more intensity than some others. That is the unique thing about the illness; not every journey is the same.

No fuel in the tank

One of the early signs of my impending illness was that I was always tired, extraordinarily lethargic, and seemed to lack enough energy to complete even the most basic of tasks. Simple things like having a shower, brushing my teeth, or getting dressed became a massive chore and overwhelming to the point that I would avoid them because these things just seemed such a hassle and too hard to accomplish.

I neglected myself for over three years. I seldom showered, shaved or brushed my hair. What I wore did not concern me. I was not going anywhere. It was too much of an ordeal. I had barely enough energy to walk around the house.

Initially, I attributed the fatigue, loss of energy and tiredness to my work. I had opened my practice in 2011. I had been working long hours for a protracted period. I felt that I could not take holidays or breaks due to the workload and the growth of the business. I was indispensable. The company could not survive without me. It needed me, surely? Sound familiar?

With the benefit of time and reflection, I would learn that this was a mistake. Being the Minister for Hindsight is not always helpful, but self-reflection is an essential skill in dealing with depression. It provides context and information about how you got there and, more importantly, can provide a guiding beacon to get you out and ensure you stay out.

Why is everything blue?

One of the most challenging aspects of depression to explain to people that have not suffered from it is the dark moods, always feeling sad, deeply and uncontrollably melancholy, and 'blue' most of the day, every day. A sustained, prolonged and painful agony that leaves you feeling empty, worthless and helpless while instilling an inescapable sense of despair, yielding darkness that tortures and torments you when it feels like it, without warning.

No matter how hard I fought against these feelings, I could not avoid them nor control when they would take over my life. Ultimately, I had to meet them head-on. It was the hardest thing that I have ever done, but it was not impossible.

All pain, no pleasure

I lost interest in activities I had once enjoyed and things that had previously pleased me no longer did so during depressive episodes.

Sex was one. During these times, I lost my mojo. I had heard from older male friends, mostly baby boomers, but also some fellow members of Generation X, that this can eventuate from the physical ageing process and sometimes required the intervention of modern pharmaceutical medicine to overcome.

Alas, it turned out that this was not yet my problem, but rather I discovered that a loss of libido was an ordinary part of the symptoms of the illness. Sunday mornings were usually the day. I had been married for almost twenty-five years. For younger readers, routine becomes increasingly important as you get older! The allocated day went by, week after week, without the same level of eager anticipation, interest, and enthusiasm that I had otherwise displayed previously. Depression had stolen one of life's most simple pleasures. For a time, it became the killjoy of marital intimacy and ruined my Sundays!

Before my diagnosis, I was an avid sports lover and enjoyed watching anything related to sport. I also enjoyed riding my jet ski out on the Broadwater of the Gold Coast in Australia and getting back to nature by going for walks through the various national parks. Reading and listening to music was something that I often did to relax and unwind. Spending time with my family and closest friends, the majority of whom I had known for over thirty years, some longer, was a significant part of my life that brought me happiness and enjoyment.

These were the things that interested me, and I enjoyed the most about my life. Depression brought an end to that. I withdrew from social contact with my friends for long periods at a time. They suspected something was wrong, but I didn't tell them about my diagnosis for several years. I no longer had an interest in watching sport, the jet ski, reading, socialising or engaging with nature.

I hated that depression had robbed me of these things. I despised the illness for inflicting its pain and depriving me of any pleasure in my life. I had to find ways of rediscovering the joys. To do so, I had to fight each symptom, one by one, until they no longer controlled my life. Until I did that, my life would be all pain, no pleasure.

Why can't I concentrate?

Another significant sign that my depression was looming was that I became easily distracted, memory recall was a challenge, and I found it incredibly difficult to concentrate on my work or in my life generally. From my perspective, this was not normal.

Over many years, my work had required a high level of concentration, memory recall, analytical thought processes, higher reasoning, and attention to detail. Being easily distracted and unable to concentrate introduced the risk of making mistakes that had the potential to cost clients' money and cause irreparable damage to long-standing relationships and professional reputations.

I started always to doubt myself. I could not seem to make decisions and avoided doing so. I lost motivation to even turn up to the office, while my staff continued to work. I found it challenging to provide them with instructions and could not face the prospect of engaging with clients for fear that my secret would leak, and I would be exposed as a failure. Eventually, the closure of my business and ceasing work for my valued employees was inevitable. I had spent the past six years establishing new relationships, enhancing long-standing ones, and growing the business. It was gut-wrenching to let it go, but I had no other choice.

The closure led to feelings of failure. I felt inadequate and incapable of performing even the most basic level of work that I had been doing for the previous twenty-five years. My self-esteem plummeted. I was at rock bottom for a long time. Other symptoms would continue to be relentless during this period in ensuring they kept me on the downward spiral of misery.

Later, as part of my recovery efforts, I embarked upon some volunteer work and further study. I started and withdrew from three separate courses. I resigned from my part-time volunteer roles in less than six months. These efforts brought back the intense feelings of failure. The lesson here was that rushing my recovery was not possible. My return to work had to wait until I was ready.

I could not function at work, which ultimately cost me a lot of money, but my recovery was worth far more. I needed to get back to being me for the benefit of myself and my family. I needed to accept that depression and anxiety had their own timetable, and that change would come through persistence and effort. It did.

Beware of the black dog!

Depression is also known as the 'black dog', the term Winston Churchill allegedly used to describe his depression. The Black Dog Institute[65] uses it as their logo to acknowledge that depression can 'shadow' the sufferer, even when their mood is upbeat and 'victorious'.[66] For those interested, there is some conjecture as to whether Winston Churchill did have depression or some other form of mental illness.[67] Still, regardless of whether he did have depression or not, the concept of the black dog is a good one. It gives the disease a real identity, something you can sense and objectify, rather than the intangible reality. Historically, it was an expression used by nannies in the Victorian era to connote the bad moods of their charges.[68] From my perspective, the idea of a black dog evoked a creature that was more of a ferocious wild beast emerging from the darkness of the shadows than a domestic pet of the best-friend variety.

People also use the black dog reference to create an image of something to fight against while they are suffering. They want to beat the black dog before it kills them—by suicide mostly. I was the same.

Thoughts of death are common in depression. It is the way you deal with these that matters. I thought about it regularly; sometimes, every day. In late 2018, I began to remind myself that I have fought for other things. For my family, my children, friends, clients, causes I believed in, even my sporting teams. I asked myself, *Why is this any different?*

Later, I developed strategies to respond to these thoughts and defend myself against their persistent attacks. One coping strategy I devised became my Miss List. I will talk about that more in Chapter Five. Suffice to say, it saved my life.

I am a failure

I felt emasculated by my inability to work and continue to generate the income that I had become accustomed to and worked hard to provide for my family. In turn, this led to deep feelings of personal failure, worthlessness, and guilt.

I began to deliberate excessively over minor past failings, brooding over unresolvable conflicts and questions that it was impossible to answer, like: *Why am I such a loser? When will this end? What do people really think of me? What is the point?* This ruminative process fed my feelings of failure, worthlessness, and guilt.

I felt like a failure because I had lost my business. I no longer had a future. I was no longer a role model to my children and someone they would be proud to emulate. I felt worthless because I could no longer provide for my family nor, at times, help them when they were in need because the illness so debilitated me. I felt guilty because I could not work, and I had allowed this illness to take over my life and so profoundly impact the lives of my immediate family.

I felt like a loser because it was taking me so long to recover from the illness, and nothing I did seemed to yield any progress. I felt shame because I always had to lie to people about my condition—my standard line was, 'Oh, I'm retired'—to hide the fact that I was no longer working because of the effects of depression. Emotionally, too, I had become a void, finding it difficult to show real love and emotion to those that cared for me the most, namely, my wife, children and closest friends. I despised myself for that.

In combination, I felt humiliated and lost all self-respect in the process. I had no self-esteem.

It became a vicious cycle.

I would learn that the feelings I held were a usual symptom of depression,[69] and rumination is a repetitive pattern of thought that plagues many patients with depression by engaging them in ideas about themselves, the future, and the social world.[70]

Adjusting the belt

Within a month or so of my diagnosis, I had put on a considerable amount of weight. Exercise had stopped altogether. Enjoying my favourite recreational activities became a thing of the past. I craved junk food, overate, and overindulged in alcohol.

I was so apathetic and down on life and my future that I just couldn't be bothered. What was the point? My self-respect had evaporated. Depression had stolen it like a common thief. Other symptoms like fatigue, loss of energy and constant tiredness did not assist. They were just fuel to the fire.

I had to claw myself from the wreckage that my mind and body had become. I had to learn strategies to cope with the effects of the symptoms. I would not resume my recovery journey until I did exactly that.

To sleep or not to sleep—that is not the question

At various stages of my illness, my sleep was affected in different ways. Sometimes it felt like I was sleeping continuously, finding it difficult to stay awake long enough to do even the most basic of things. At other times, I just could not sleep. I would lie in bed most of the night, crying a lot and wishing that the dark thoughts running through my head would abate long enough for my brain to think it was safe to sleep.

I had no control over my sleep. It was something that I came to fear, especially in the silence of night when there is nothing but the quiet—no distractions, no noises of household appliances, people talking or movement outside. Being victim to your thoughts for long periods almost every day feeds other symptoms and keeps them alive. Tiredness, fatigue and loss of energy were good examples. Thoughts of death beyond ordinary contemplation of dying was another. To sleep or not to sleep—that was not the question. Rather, it was, *How do I keep these beasts at bay?*

Mountains from molehills

Unexpected anger and irritability were frequent visitors to my thoughts and feelings during depression. Sometimes it would be intense; other times, moderate but still pervasive. Little things that would usually have passed without a grimace now became the mountains where the molehills once stood.

I also felt resentment for the illness, which fuelled my anger. I was angry because it picked me and made me feel the way it did. I resented the impact my illness had on my wife and children and how it took me away from my friends. I was angry because I did not know how I got it. I certainly didn't ask for it. Nor was I looking for it. All I knew was that it wasn't invited and needed to go away. The only way it was ever going to do that was if I fought it in the way nature intended— fight or flight—I had to learn how to be the bigger dog.

Enter anxiety

While not a symptom of depression, I also developed anxiety. Withdrawing from friends was one effect of depression, but anxiety took this to a new level.

With anxiety, I would feel tense, wound up and edgy every time I had to leave the house. I avoided social situations consistently because I worried that my symptoms and their effects would lead to embarrassment or be perceived negatively by others. I would not use public transport, avoided being in enclosed spaces, standing in line or being in a crowd and being outside the home alone. I constantly worried about several aspects of everyday life (way more than usual), including work, health, family, and financial issues, rather than just one problem at a time.

Specific dates and activities triggered anxiety. The anniversary date of my diagnosis was one example. Activities like visiting the suburb where my offices had been or places where my former work colleagues might gather were also problematic. I agonised over the prospect of meeting someone from my 'past'. I was fearful of having to explain my position and suffering the indignity and embarrassment that I felt sure would follow any conversation around this topic. I learned that my concerns were a regular part of having anxiety. Anniversary dates of traumatic events, for example, can reactivate thoughts and feelings from the actual incident and survivors may experience peaks of anxiety and depression.[71] I needed to learn to cope with these situations—this required time.

Anxiety disorders can coexist with depression[72] to the point that the occurrence of one disease may be a predisposing factor for developing the other.[73] Having both anxiety and depression increases the severity and number of symptoms of each condition, resulting in more significant impairment.[74] Some of the symptoms of anxiety and depression also overlap. Overthinking, avoidance, sleep disturbance,[75] irritability and difficulty concentrating are examples.

Anxiety is the most common health problem in Australia. On average, one in four people—one in three women and one in five men—will experience anxiety at some stage of their life.[76] Globally, the proportion of the population with anxiety disorders is estimated to be 3.6 per cent.[77]

Once again, I learned that I was not alone. The coping strategies that I had developed and utilised concerning depression would not go to waste when anxiety came along.

ROBERT NICHOLLS

CHAPTER THREE: BARRIERS TO TREATMENT

*A hero is an ordinary individual who finds the strength to
persevere and endure
in spite of overwhelming obstacles.*
— CHRISTOPHER REEVE

Obstacles exist that will make your journey more difficult than it should be. You should acquaint yourself with these and prepare for them—they are the barriers to treatment. These barriers can obscure the pathways to your recovery.

Common barriers to effective care include a lack of resources, lack of trained health care providers and social stigma associated with mental disorders.[78] To this list, I would add the symptoms, which can themselves become barriers, and the willingness of the sufferer to take the first steps towards recovery (which I outline in Chapter Four).

Back to the railway station

Today, I can still remember the reaction of people trying to get to work that morning at Newtown Railway Station. It was a ten-minute train trip into the Sydney CBD. Buses went there too. Back then, I didn't understand why these people could not have walked around the corner and hopped on a bus to work instead. Perhaps the bus trip was longer!

I recall informing commuters that a young man had lost his life while suffering from the effects of depression, and the station would be closed for some time. The reaction of those people has stayed with me. They were visibly upset, angry, frustrated and wanted to make it clear to police that they were being inconvenienced by not being able to get to work on time. It was evident they didn't want to take the time to understand what it had been like for that young man, suffering as he must have been to the point of opting to end his own life. On reflection, I know today that some of the commuters from that day, like many people in society, were just ignorant about depression.

Nothing has changed. Be prepared for the same attitudes from people. Do not be surprised if some of these people may be your family, friends, or work colleagues. There is nothing you can do about it. Just accept it and focus your energy on aspects of your recovery that you can control, like your willingness to accept change and be flexible in the approach to your treatment and recovery.

Stigma

Apart from the obvious suffering endured by people with depression and anxiety, sufferers also have to deal with the misconceptions that still exist about mental health problems.[79] The most common fallacies are that there is no treatment for mental health problems; mental health problems are caused by personal weaknesses; that people with mental disorders are incapable of making decisions for themselves or running their own lives; and that people with depression can't be trusted to work alongside others. Misconceptions like these yield a stigma regarding mental illness and those suffering from it.

Stigma is a significant issue in mental health: it lowers people's self-esteem, makes symptoms more severe and limits help-seeking behaviours.[80] Depression may also be accompanied by discrimination.[81]

At times, the stigma can feel worse than the illness itself. It presents in many guises. Ignorance or misinformation, prejudice, and outright discrimination are its main components.[82] While it generally comes from other people, even family and friends, stigma can also permeate your consciousness through a mistaken belief that you should be able to snap out of your depression. Unfortunately, there is no switch to turn it off and on. It runs with or without your co-operation.

Beyond Blue reports that the two most effective approaches to reducing stigma are education and contact (including personal contact with people with depression and anxiety).[83]

In my view, stigma will continue to exist for as long as there are ignorant, prejudiced, and poorly behaved people in the world. These people are not important to your journey. They will only extend it. Cast them aside and consign them to history. Only invite members of your family and friends that are prepared to gain the knowledge about the illness, refuse to adopt prejudicial attitudes, and avoid the behaviour that is discrimination.

You may think that friends or members of your own family would never stigmatise your illness. I thought the same thing. Family are supposed to be there for you unconditionally. Friends are expected to be loyal and supportive, especially when you go through hard times. It doesn't always work out that way and it is vital to accept that. Depression is a journey like any other in life. You are likely to go through it with the people that are the closest to you at that time. You may be surprised by who those people are, and who they are not.

Society is unforgiving. In 2020, there is still a stigma attached to the illness and there should not be. I am not sure whether my career prospects will be affected by writing this book. More than likely they will, but I am prepared to take that risk. Leaders need to take responsibility in this area and dispel the myths surrounding the illness, namely, that it is a weakness, there is something wrong with people suffering from it or that people with depression can't be trusted to work alongside others.

Workplaces are not exempt from societal tendencies towards mental health stigma. A recent Australian study revealed that about one in three people had reservations about working with someone experiencing depression or anxiety; preferred that their supervisor or manager did not have these illnesses; and did not think a co-worker with depression or anxiety would be capable of performing their job adequately.[84]

The same study also reported that most employees would not disclose their experience of a mental health condition within their workplace. The study cited a reluctance by employees to disclose their experience of depression to employers due to a lack of support for mental health by line managers, the CEO, or their industry.[85]

According to mental health advocate Ruby Wax,[86] 'If you become mentally ill, don't – whatever you do – tell your boss.'[87] She explains it this way:

> *When people say, 'Should you tell them at work?', I say: 'Are you crazy?' You have to lie. If you have someone who is physically ill, they can't fire you. They can't fire you for mental health problems, but they'll say it's for another reason. Mental illness is like the situation used*

to be with gay rights. Like being in the closet, but mental illness is now the taboo instead.[88]

Ruby is right. Globally, while there is more awareness, more advertising, and a growing amount of assistance to people suffering from mental illness, societal attitudes and acceptance have not caught up. As a society, we have changed our opinions about a whole range of subjects previously considered taboo, like gay marriage and racial discrimination. While we may have a long way to go in these areas as well, at least we have shifted, made a decisive move toward change. With depression, I am uncertain that I will see the same shift in my lifetime, but I remain hopeful that it will come. Acceptance, compassion, tolerance, and respect will alleviate a significant amount of needless suffering. The sooner it happens, the better.

There are no shortages of examples of high-profile people prepared to disclose their mental health issues. Sporting stars, politicians, movie stars and TV personalities have all confessed publicly to being vulnerable and exposed to the effects of depression and anxiety. Yet, people still don't seem to understand it, or at least be willing to accept it. It remains taboo.

If society was accepting of mental illness—I mean genuinely accepting—we would have more of our business and political leaders leading the way in this area. It's about time they stood up and did exactly that.

Perceptions become a reality

During your illness, you might hear or become aware of people, as I did, say things like:

Dave should just get over it and move on.

Jane is depressed. She just can't hack it.
Mick can't handle the pressure.
Depression is for those that think there's something
wrong but don't know what it is.
Sarah is just unhappy. She can't be depressed.

Unfortunately, these people may be from within your family, one of your friends or work colleagues.

If you ever hear these things, just know that the people who utter these words are ignorant and their comments ill-informed, misguided, and wrong. As hard as it may be at times for you to cast these aside, you must remember that (at the present day at least) no one can read your mind and know precisely what you are going through. The logical reasoning from that fact (and the good news) is that the cure for your mental illness lies within you. It's in there.

For some people, perception is reality, even if ignorance feeds it. Ignorance comes from a lack of understanding. A lack of understanding derives its force from an absence of knowledge. The key to resolving ignorance is, therefore, knowledge. If somebody doesn't understand something or perceives things a certain way, it is sometimes better to allow them an opportunity (or time) to educate themselves so that they can be part of your Recovery Team (more on that later). The other option is to leave them behind. That process may hurt, but it is sometimes necessary for you to progress on your journey. You can always reunite later if the circumstances permit because, as I intimated earlier, this illness will reveal who your 'real' friends and carers are (and who they are not).

Symptoms as barriers

Unlike a broken arm, the insidious part of depression is that it takes away the drive to get treatment.[89] Your symptoms become a barrier.

I found that depression was always hungry. It always fed itself. Every time I tried to motivate myself to deal with my symptoms—by exercising, for example—it would pull me under and consume me to the point where I felt unable to because symptoms like the constant fatigue, lethargy, lack of motivation and others took over. I was always 'going to'. It became a vicious cycle. One in which it seemed like each of the symptoms was fighting against one another for prominence. All my symptoms were co-existing and preventing me from taking the necessary steps towards my recovery.

The barriers to effective treatment impact the willingness of a sufferer to seek out care and support.[90] They prevent the taking of the critical first steps (discussed in the next chapter) and have the capacity to end your recovery journey before it even has a chance to begin.

Adequacy of support

Support is critical to recovery from depression. It can come from a variety of sources, including doctors, specialist nurses, mental health practitioners, support groups, friends, and family—your Recovery Team. You must adjudge the adequacy of this support. You will know when your support network is working or when one of your Recovery Team members is not performing and needs to be replaced. Starting the process of building your support network often begins with your commitment to attend your GP.

In Australia, depression and anxiety have been reported to be more common than coughs and colds,[91] with research finding that one in eight visits to GPs is related to mental health issues.[92] This research highlights a national trend evidencing that support seeking is growing at a rapid rate. Almost half of all people with a condition are now getting treatment.[93]

Evidence also indicates men are far less likely to seek help for mental health conditions than women. According to the National Survey of Mental Health and Wellbeing (2007) study, only 27.5 per cent of males with a mental disorder and recent symptoms had accessed services for their mental health problems compared with 40.7 per cent of females.[94]

Seeking support can assist you in overcoming barriers to treatment by taking the all-important first steps that can mitigate against the risk of sabotage caused by inadequate care or other obstacles, and encourage you to start to establish your Recovery Team.

In Chapter Six, I will talk about how to go about selecting the team members for your Recovery Team, and in Chapter Seven, I offer some tips to carers and supporters on how they can be a useful part of that team.

Lack of resources

Depending on the severity of your symptoms, you may not be able to work for some time, which influences your ability to generate money to get treatment or to seek it out as frequently as you would like to or need it. A lack of financial resources can be a significant impediment to your recovery pathways. Most countries around the world have subsidised treatment options.

You should speak to your GP or mental health practitioners about these options. Support groups are also an effective means of learning about available funding and treatment options that do not require significant financial resources.

ROBERT NICHOLLS

CHAPTER FOUR: NO PAIN. NO GAIN.

The fight is won or lost far away from witnesses – behind the lines, in the gym, and out there on the road, long before I dance under those lights.

— MUHAMMAD ALI

Traditional treatments for depression are prescription antidepressant medications[95] and non-medical alternatives of support from health professionals,[96] community or organisation-based support networks,[97] types of therapy[98] and changes in lifestyle choices such as diet[99] and exercise.[100] Self-help approaches and counselling have also proved effective psychological interventions for depression.[101]

For most people, it will be a combination of these that will prove to be effective in the treatment of depression.[102]

Treatment and support for depression can come from many health professionals in primary or secondary care, depending on the severity of symptoms. Mental health nurses, GPs, occupational therapists, psychologists, and psychiatrists can all provide evidence-based interventions.[103]

Medications

Antidepressants are medicines that treat depression. According to the National Institute of Mental Health,[104] these medications may help improve the way your brain uses certain chemicals that control mood or stress. You may need to try several different antidepressant medicines before finding the one that improves your symptoms and has manageable side effects.[105]

I was never a major fan of anti-depressant medication, mostly due to the side effects that I experienced while taking them, particularly headaches and weight gain. In my situation, I found that these and other medication-specific side effects outweighed the benefits and did not provide the same advantages that I received from other forms of treatment, and so, for me, the medicines would not form as significant a part in my recovery journey. However, I did find them of more probative value during major depressive episodes.

Your situation may be different. Before you commence or discontinue any medication, you should always consult your doctor to seek advice that is appropriate to your circumstances.

Psychotherapies

Psychotherapy is one of the most effective treatments for all types of depression and has very few side effects.[106] Both technology-assisted and face-to-face therapy are effective.[107]

Cognitive-behavioural therapy (CBT), interpersonal therapy, and psychodynamic therapy are psychotherapy approaches scientifically proven to work with depression.[108]

For mild depression, many people start with self-help strategies and emotional support.[109] There are some conventional herbal treatments that research has also shown to be effective, including St. John's wort,[110] although serious concerns exist about its safety and questions remain about the veracity of the claims made about its effectiveness.[111] Dietary supplements, including omega-3 fatty acids and others, remain under study but have similarly not been proven safe and effective for routine use.[112]

Electroconvulsive therapy may be used for severe depression. Despite controversy about the treatment, due to misconceptions or unfamiliarity, it is acknowledged to be one of the most effective treatments for severe mood disorders.[113]

Exercise and lifestyle choices

Although psychoeducation,[114] medication and psychological approaches are effective in treating depression,[115] regular exercise may be an essential component of treatment for all severity levels of the illness.[116]

Maintaining good mental health can also be achieved through the adoption of several lifestyle approaches,[117] including making connections with other people, eating well,[118] taking breaks when required and drinking alcohol within recommended limits.[119] According to research, these approaches improve symptoms.[120]

The keys to successful treatment

When I was first diagnosed, I thought I could just deal with the illness myself. Take treatment into my own hands and work some miracle cure to get me back on track with my 'normal' life.

I surmised there would be a 'standard' way of getting better. I was wrong. No two people are affected the same way by depression, and there is no 'one-size-fits-all' for treatment.[121] It will take some trial and error to find the treatment that works best for you.[122] Once you have done so, it will be the 'right' treatment.

My initial response was a mistake, but ultimately, it also provided valuable learning that became critical to my recovery efforts. The error in my approach was that it failed to acknowledge the need for me to, firstly, recognise and accept that I had a serious problem. Next, I needed treatment and support from other people to help me recover, and a treatment plan to follow to get me there, even if that plan changed from time to time.

The valuable lesson I learned was that if my treatment was to be effective, I had to own it. I had to be the driver, not a passenger, in my recovery, regardless of which treatment options were available. It is critical to take this first step and then to be actively involved in the direction of your treatment. Research indicates it is the most effective way to promote recovery from mental illness.[123]

This approach can be far more challenging for someone who is depressed than it sounds. Finding the motivation to exercise, for example, can be incredibly difficult and frustrating to accomplish. Depression starves you of the stimulus and energy required to move and makes basic things like brushing your teeth seem like a huge obstacle and, at times, an impossible task. Consequently, patience is a core necessity when starting treatment.[124] Small steps are also required, and each one should be acknowledged (even celebrated) as an accomplishment. Be prepared for setbacks but understand that without commitment to your recovery process—without some pain—there will be no gain.

In Chapter 3, I highlighted some barriers to treatment and discussed how these obstacles inhibit support seeking and impede effective recovery processes. In my experience, the other key to successful treatment is to acknowledge these barriers and form an understanding of how they may be affecting your treatment and recovery journey. Once you have done so, it is essential to make any necessary adjustments, including developing strategies to respond to these hurdles. I will introduce some coping strategies in Chapter Five.

While experiencing the effects of depression, you may feel like the options presented in this chapter are not only unattractive but, at times, seem aspirational and unattainable. It is essential during these periods to remind yourself that although depression is a chronic condition that can recur throughout life,[125] it does not have to mean a state of consistent suffering and powerlessness but, instead, a journey that includes setbacks and successes.[126]

Just remember to always be in the driver's seat.

CHAPTER FIVE: COPING STRATEGIES

Rivers know this: there is no hurry. We shall get there some day.
— A.A. MILNE, WINNIE-THE-POOH

You need to develop strategies for coping with depression. Without these strategies, your journey to recovery is likely to be delayed substantially. I will now share the coping strategies that worked for me. You will learn to develop your own alongside some or all of those that I will introduce to you.

The coping strategies I developed and learned did not come to me overnight. They were formed in the process of enduring several years of thought-provoking agony, a lot of pain and suffering and by continually asking questions about myself and the effects the illness was having upon me, then consistently searching for answers.

Once depression takes its grip, it doesn't let go voluntarily. It will torment you. And will more than likely bring you to your knees. I was debilitated and helpless for a long time. Every day was a struggle. At times, I thought I was beaten.

Gradually, I developed some rules and mantras that I would adhere to in my response to depression. Sticking to these allowed me to respond to unexpected issues and avoid the worsening of symptoms in stressful situations or when these were at their worst. I also learned some valuable lessons from others and adapted these to my situation.

Coping strategies that worked

Here are some coping strategies that worked for me at various times during my battle with depression and anxiety. Not all the time or every time but at critical moments in my journey.

The key to developing effective coping strategies is to accept that there is no fixed menu of options. Be prepared to try and retry different approaches at varying intervals in your pathway because timing can be critical. Perseverance is a must. Don't be deterred if a strategy doesn't work for you the first time. It might take the second, third or tenth time. It doesn't matter when. It matters how effective it is when you need it most. Also, be patient. Effective coping strategies take time to evolve.

Fight or flight

Think about something that you have felt passionately about in your life before your illness. Something you have fought for before because you believed in the cause and thought it was the right thing to do. Dealing with depression is the same. It is not right for you to have to deal with it, to live with it and to suffer by it, so do something about it. Fight it. Defend yourself.

Do whatever you need to do to deal with the illness in your unique way. You will be in for a fight, but you can win it. Believe in yourself, be patient and invest the time.

Be prepared for change

Be prepared for change, or at least the need to adapt to change, whether as a consequence of your change in financial position, relationships, emotional standing or any other reason that might arise from you having the illness and taking steps to overcome it. This approach is important because change is inevitable. You will never be the same person that you were before your illness, but you have an opportunity to be a better one. By accepting the need to be flexible in your approach, and that change is inevitable if you are to recover from the illness, your journey is likely to become more manageable.

The Miss List

I found this useful when I was confronting thoughts of death during my darkest episodes of depression. Like a wish list or to-do list, I developed a *Miss List*—a list of things that I would miss if I took my own life. Watching my children become adults, get their first jobs, becoming a grandfather, getting hugs from my kids and love from my wife, sharing laughs with close friends, the ocean, riding my jet ski, listening to music and the smell of grass after mowing the lawns were some of mine.

I would keep the list close by and pull it out every time I had these thoughts. I kept adding to it. It was not a definitive list. In many ways, it was potentially endless. The longer it grew, the more reasons I gave myself to stay and stick it out. It worked.

Name your villain

When I spoke or thought about depression, I did so with venom. I gave my illness a persona, something that I could be angry with, show my resentment to, despise, fight against, so that I could defeat it. My nemesis, if you like. In this way, I was able to divorce it from the 'real' me and make it something temporary rather than a fixture. I made it feel unwelcome and reminded it consistently that it was no friend of mine. This approach gave me the incentive to fight.

Turn pro

Think about the way a professional athlete or business leader goes about their business methodically, systematically and with the professionalism engendered by a belief in their skills, ability and preparation. Perfect practice is the key. This belief is also a way of approaching your depression.

In other words, you need to turn pro. I approached my depression as though it were a problem like any other that I have dealt with in my working life. It became a project. Recovery was the deliverable. By doing this, I was able to give some objectivity to the process, and this made it easier for me to take away the personal influences and effect that the illness was having upon me.

Follow a hero

We all have heroes in our lives. People we admire and respect for the way they go about their sport, trade or profession, their level of accomplishment, the ways they respond to pressure or fame. People we look up to, aspire to be like and are willing to support publicly to the exclusion of all their contemporaries.

Identify your hero or heroes. Every time you get stuck on your journey or a pathway, ask yourself, *What would my hero do if faced with the same or similar choice or predicament? How would they approach it? What are the qualities in them that make them so strong and capable of finding solutions to their problems and issues?* Copy the approach you think your hero would take or the choices you think they would make to get ahead of the game.

My heroes were tennis legend Roger Federer, and Australian cricketer Steve Smith. I admired these men for different reasons.

Roger Federer is the consummate professional. He is calm under pressure, never gives up and is always as humble in victory as he is in defeat. A fierce competitor that never displays aggression towards his opponent, only respect. He lets his prowess with the racquet do the talking. If that fails, he never blames anybody else. He owns his decisions. He takes charge of the things that he can control. His achievements speak for themselves.

Steve Smith is one of the best batsmen the world has ever seen. His transgressions as captain of the Australian Cricket Team while on tour in South Africa in March 2018, the so-called *Sandpapergate* scandal, brought him to his knees. While he took ownership of the leadership blunder perpetrated by him, he paid the ultimate price in the form of a one-year ban from the game he loved. He lost the captaincy and the kudos and money that goes with being in the position he was before the scandal. More importantly, he also lost the respect of the cricket world and Australian fans. The courage, grit, tenacity, and determination, however, that Steve Smith showed in returning to the Australian Cricket Team on their tour to England in 2019 was nothing short of phenomenal. Overcoming the chants, derogatory remarks and rhetoric of the English fans, and beating after beating by the English press, Smith walked onto Edgbaston Cricket Ground and dominated with the bat, scoring 144 and 142, earning him the Man of the Match title, and steering Australia to victory in the test. Records would tumble in that test series, and Steve Smith was restored to his place of eminence amongst the cricketing fraternity and earned renewed respect from fans, teammates, and opponents alike.

Every time I came to a point in my journey where I thought I might be beaten, I thought about Roger Federer and Steve Smith, drawing inspiration from the way they approach their games, overcome obstacles and rise above it all to be the world-class champions they are. Eventually, these heroes would help me rise above depression and to take control of my direction and pathways to recovery.

Find your song
During some of my darkest episodes of depression in 2018, Shawn Mendes released a song called 'In My Blood'. This song and its messages are significant in my journey because it came at a time when I needed it most and provided constant inspiration for me to maintain my fight with the illness.

Every time my mind wanted to take me somewhere dark and morbid, I would play the song. It would challenge me to stand up, continue to defend myself from the spurs of the illness and to keep going. It contributed to saving my life.

Find your song.

Immerse yourself in good memories
At times, I found it beneficial to immerse myself in good memories—something that brought joy in the past—like getting married, the birth of my kids or travelling overseas. I would look at photos or videos of these events to provide assurance that my life has had some good times in it. Great times.

Another strategy I have used in this context is to watch one of my team's victories in the sporting arena. The Australian Wallabies Rugby World Cup wins in 1991 and 1999. The Cronulla-Sutherland Sharks grand final win in 2016.

The Sharks were my local team growing up in the southern outskirts of Sydney. Watching their only grand final win since their inception in 1967 brought back some other good memories of growing up, hanging out with my friends and the simplicity of life when you are younger. It was an excellent reminder to try to keep things as simple as possible and to bring my life, and the pathways I was taking, back to the basics.

Do not expect too much too soon
I wanted to rush my recovery so that I could get back to work. I learned that depression takes its course, and no matter how hard you try, your recovery just takes time. There is no set time limit. It takes the time it needs for you to heal, and that is the 'right' amount of time.

The message here is to set realistic goals for yourself and to expect your mood to improve gradually, not immediately. This process will involve you respecting the illness and recognising the impact that it is having on your life.

By respect, I mean give it the time that it deserves, the seriousness it commands, and the commitment to making yourself better. By giving it the time, I mean taking the time out to deal with the issues that you're facing, time to consult with appropriate health professionals, time to do the things that you need to do to make yourself better. Unless and until you do that, you will always have unreasonable expectations and be incapable of establishing realistic objectives for your recovery.

Set limits
Depression makes you feel utterly exhausted and lethargic, so conserve your energy and be prepared to exclude events or people from your life that make you waste the little energy you have left to make changes and feel better.

Depression can be a vicious cycle because its symptoms interact with each other to perpetuate the effects of the illness. For example, if you waste your energy on people that are unsupportive or try to meet their unreasonable expectations while you are suffering, you will end up burnt out and resentful. In turn, this leaves you with nothing in the tank to keep fighting your own battle and provides fuel for other symptoms to emerge or increase in their severity. It's hard enough fighting with one hand tied; don't allow your other hand to join it in the process. Be prepared to say 'no' when you need to or to protect your recovery process.

Own your feelings
I often felt guilty about how I felt. In hindsight, this was wrong, but when you are suffering, you become your own worst enemy. During episodes of depression, it is possible to morph as a master of deprecation—a minister of self-hatred.

Later in my journey, I realised that my feelings were the one thing that depression could not take away. Yes, the illness could influence them, it could change them and increase their severity, but it could not take them away altogether. They were mine, which meant that if I did things to change the way I felt by becoming the driver, not the passenger, in my recovery, depression lost a little bit more of its power over me and became a weaker influence on my future wellbeing.

No one is entitled to judge you for how you feel or to criticise you for thinking or feeling a certain way. There may be some people that try, but your feelings can never be wrong. Own them and learn to understand them. Ultimately, they will become an essential piece in the puzzle of your recovery.

Smaller is better
Depression is a big thing, so it is helpful to break it up into smaller pieces. Isolating your thoughts allows you to deal with them in a piecemeal fashion, like putting a jigsaw together, one

part of the jigsaw at a time. In the end, you will have completed the whole jigsaw puzzle. Your thought processes must be the same: focus on one issue, think about it, deal with it, respond to it, then move onto the next. It is also essential when you do so to take the time to celebrate your successes in dealing with these individual issues. Reward yourself with a favourite meal or some other indulgence. It will make you feel better, but more critically, it will allow you to make progress.

Re-evaluate your options
There will be times throughout your journey when you have opportunities to evaluate your progress. Use these to assess the progress you are making towards your recovery and your future life. These are valuable opportunities because they can provide constructive feedback about your journey and its future direction.

During these times, ask yourself a lot of questions like: *Do I need to change my pathway? Have the strategies I have used been working? Are there others that I can use? When I recover, how do I prevent a relapse? Do I need to change anything about me or my life to make my recovery a permanent thing?*

Use the time to try to be more objective about where you are at in life. It is an opportunity to question everything and accept nothing. Clean the slate. Start over. There is nothing wrong with that. Seize these moments to try to find meaning and explore prospects for you to restore hope to your life. For some people, that might be religion. For others, philanthropy, or a change in career. It does not matter what it is; the critical aspect is the restoration of hope because depression steals it away and holds you captive to it. Once hope returns, depression starts to die.

Find a good listener

Finding a good listener to be a member of your Recovery Team is critical to your progress and your ultimate recovery from depression. They don't have to be a qualified health professional or experienced in depression or anxiety treatment. If you can find someone capable of listening, understanding and offering general support, this can be of great assistance in dealing with the day to day implications of these illnesses and in your pathways to recovery.

Write something. Anything!

I can't take all the credit for this book coming into existence. My therapist suggested it. It was a great idea. I found it to be a powerful way to process my thoughts and feelings and ease my depression. It doesn't matter what you write. Just start, and it tends to take over. Unless you want them to, no one else has to read it. Writing should always be about you first, others second or not at all.

Read

It sounds logical that if writing is likely to assist you, reading will too. Depression can impair your ability to concentrate. At times when you find that you can focus, you might be able to read, even if it is a few lines, a page or chapter. Self-help books can be useful. So, too, an opportunity to lose yourself in fiction. Reading helped me to educate myself about depression and anxiety and afforded me the luxury of escaping my world.

Keep moving

Depression can deprive you of the energy and motivation to exercise, but there is an abundance of research supporting its positive impact on recovery. My advice is to start with small steps and gradually build as you progress through the illness. Don't punish yourself if you don't stick to your exercise plan all the time. Accept that there will be days when you simply cannot make it because the effect of your symptoms outweighs your desire to make progress in this aspect of your treatment. Just keep persevering to keep moving.

Engage with nature

Sir David Attenborough once said that he knew of 'no pleasure deeper than that which comes from contemplating the natural world and trying to understand it'. Engaging with nature as part of your treatment for depression has many benefits. It provides an opportunity to gain perspective and to appreciate simplicity. These outcomes are critical to your recovery.

When you are immersed in a depressive episode, the world, and your existence in it feels like it is incredibly complicated, your symptoms control you and your time is devoted continuously to your battle with the illness. You can feel like you are going to explode from the pressure imposed from the confines of your head and your room. It can be easy to lose sight of pathways lying in front of you and difficult to break free from the shackles of depression.

It is like catching a plane from one destination to another. As you travel over the water and the ground below at approximately 900 kilometres per hour, you never see everything beneath you. You have no control over that. The plane dictates your direction, how and when you will get to your destination.

Taking time out now and then to enjoy the simplicity of nature can give you back control and provide perspective about where you are and what you are doing. Simple things like watching and listening to waves crashing onto rocks or rolling gently onto the shore and the playful, innocent interaction between animals can serve to alleviate the complexity that comes with depression and anxiety, providing an opportunity for clarity and focus. It can yield direction, a renewed sense of belonging to the world and give you purpose. It can also teach you that approaching your life, your problems, and your illness with the absolute simplicity that nature offers can be beneficial in discovering your pathways to recovery from depression.

Feeding your senses, restoring belief, and stimulating your perspective is essential. You need to open your door, walk outside, watch, and listen. Get some sun and breathe fresh air. Listen to nature. It is calling and asking for nothing in return but your admiration—a good investment of your time and energy.

Reflection

When we drive a car, we glance in the rear-view mirror to see what is behind us and assess approaching traffic. The mirrors allow us to determine where we have come from, to avoid collisions and remind us of the progress that has been made in our journey. Returning our gaze forward restores our focus on the journey ahead.

In the same way, reflecting on our pathways during depression can be a valuable exercise in gaining perspective and clarity on our trip home to recovery.

In Chapter Two, I observed that reflection is a critical skill in dealing with depression. It provides context and information about how you got there and, more importantly, can provide a guiding beacon to get you out and help you stay out. While maintaining your focus is critical on the journey ahead, occasionally glancing in your rear-view mirror will give you the confidence that you can make it the rest of the way home.

Be selfish

Making yourself the primary focus during recovery can be problematic. As parents, guardians, or carers, we are used to placing the interests of others above our own. Looking after our flock—it is human nature.

However, recovery from depression requires your full focus and attention, which necessitates the uncomfortable prospect of making it all about you. This process may involve addressing your needs before you attend to those of others accustomed to you being there for them. Taking time out to pursue steps in your treatment plan, which may not involve those closest to you, particularly young children, is incredibly hard but necessary if you are to seek redemption from the illness.

Inviting your loved ones to be members of your Recovery Team and to take part in your journey in other ways may be one way of resolving this internal conflict and restoring some balance to the household.

Take ownership

Last but certainly not least, be the driver, not a passenger, in your journey. I repeat this message several times in this book because you must control the direction of your treatment and recovery. That doesn't mean you don't need support; you do. It also doesn't mean that you should not be guided and assisted wherever possible by your Recovery Team; you should. The point is that therapy sessions, for example, only last for about an hour. After that, you are on your own. So rather than waiting until the next meeting, take the wheel, do your homework and assume responsibility for the management of your illness and, more importantly, your recovery from it.

Important lessons learned

The world will not stop just because you have depression. The sun will still rise and set. The earth will still rotate on its axis. This fact can be a hard thing to accept when your world is collapsing around you, and it seems like doomsday has arrived on your doorstep. Some of life's everyday events can become an obstacle or set-back to recovery. Be prepared. Here are some key things I learned during my journey.

Life events do not stop
You are likely not to appreciate it at the time, but, inevitably, life will always go on around you while you are suffering from depression.

In 2018, while I was suffering from a major depressive episode, my father and nephew died; one from unknown causes in May, the other in tragic circumstances in July.

For most of my life, I was estranged from my father. When I heard he had passed away, it had a devastating effect on me. I was at such a vulnerable stage of my illness. It made me feel numb. I also felt ashamed because I felt nothing for him. I cried, but it was not a measure of the profound loss that you usually feel when someone you care about has passed away; it was because I thought that I had been a failure as a son. I was angry that I had not been able to say goodbye, and he had robbed me of that opportunity when I already felt worthless. Depression had placed the blame and guilt at my feet. It hurt more than it should have.

Several months later, my wife's nephew died tragically. He was in his early twenties. The circumstances of his death brought back memories of Newtown Railway Station twenty-eight years earlier. It broke me. To make it worse, I could not attend his funeral. Depression and anxiety had me in the worst state of my life. Once again, I felt like I had been a failure because I could not be there to comfort my family. I couldn't be there to say goodbye to my nephew. The pain and guilt orchestrated by depression continued.

While your mind continues its torment, the physical part of your existence reminds you that it will not be outdone by your mental illness. The physical aspect of your being still functions. Parts generally still work but things can still go wrong. Your physical side doesn't say, *Oh, you have a mental illness. I'll cut you some slack and leave you alone for a while.*

Unrelated to my mental illness, I had two trips to hospital.

The first one was in late September 2019. It was just after my fiftieth birthday and marked my inaugural visit (apart from the day I was born) for overnight stays in hospital and my first time as a patient in an ambulance. I had been suffering from excruciating burning pain in my upper abdomen, felt extreme nausea, and had started to hyperventilate. It was the worst pain that I had experienced. I have a high pain tolerance, but this was enough for me to beg for an ambulance. Before I was escorted from my home by the paramedics, my heart rate had started to fluctuate significantly for no apparent reason.

After several nights and numerous tests on my heart and an internal examination of my oesophagus, stomach and duodenum (upper part of the small bowel)—an endoscopy—I was treated for severe gastritis and allowed to leave the hospital with some medication and a referral to a cardiologist. Later, following more tests with the cardiologists, my heart was given the all clear and I was told I could come back in a decade or so. Good news.

It is not often during depression that you experience something that makes you laugh. It is crucial that you reflect on these moments as a sign that there is hope for your recovery from the illness even when these occasions present in unusual ways.

Before my first visit to hospital, I thought that upselling was something that they only did at McDonald's but apparently doctors also practise it. Before my endoscopy procedure, the doctor tried to upsell me a colonoscopy—she advised me that these should be done regularly after you reach fifty years of age. I resisted the offer for two reasons, which I outlined to the doctor. First, I had no pains or issues in that part of my body (as far as I was aware). Second, I thought it was a little unfair that I had only had a couple of weeks as a quinquagenarian (someone over the age of fifty but under sixty) and needed more time to reflect on the description of the procedure that she had just given me!

Perhaps due to my quirky sense of humour, I found this situation and my exchanges with the doctor amusing, although I understood that she was quite serious and ultimately turned out to be absolutely right for asking.

In January 2020, I was back in hospital. This time for the colonoscopy that I had been offered on my last visit. I should have upsized! Between hospital visits, I'd had a negative test on a bowel screen and my doctor sent me off to a specialist. It was back to hospital for another procedure. It turned out to be my lucky day because I had several large polyps removed that could potentially have yielded cancer without the timely detection arising from the short, painless procedure.

This was another time to reflect on life. I am not superstitious, but I do believe that things often happen for a reason. I realised on that day that our lives are undeniably short and constantly at the mercy of good fortune. Every positive outcome needed to be celebrated with a renewed enthusiasm for life and, with that, recovery from depression and anxiety.

The point of these stories is that there is nothing you can do to prevent life from continuing around you, and it causing pain and suffering to you and everyone you care about in the world.

Depression doesn't care how you feel when these events take place. There is no holiday from depression. There will always be life events that will drag you down, kick you in the guts and leave you begging for relief from the way you are feeling. There is nothing that you can do about this and no way to control their influence.

However, there will also be unpredictable moments when you are reminded of your sense of humour, your humanity, and the person you were before your illness. These are messages of hope. Seize the opportunity they present. Reflect and act on them in a positive way. Sometimes, there will also be events that provide you with a reprieve, even momentarily, from the illness. These are the occasions that provide opportunities for rediscovering the hope vital to your recovery. It is crucial to learn how to harness these in a constructive way.

The important thing to remember is to celebrate these glimpses of hope in whatever way suits you because, like your recovery pathway, the way you choose to revel will be the right way for you and a step towards your recovery. Treat yourself to a nice meal, some new clothes or anything that you consider an indulgence to make you feel like you are rewarding yourself for the positive experience.

Allow these events to provide you with perspective. They allow you to appreciate our frailty as human beings and accept that your pathway is open for you to navigate. These life events will come when you least expect them. The timing will always be wrong, but it is essential to understand that this is beyond anyone's control. You need to focus on things that you can control. One of these things is your pathway to recovery.

Do not be afraid to ask for help
Always keep in mind, there are people around you that care and qualified professionals that can provide therapy and support. I discovered that the people close to me were just waiting for me to ask because they weren't sure what they could do even though they wanted to help in some way. This situation is not unusual. So, don't be afraid to reach out and ask for help when you need it. Try to spend time with other people and confide in a trusted friend or relative. Try not to isolate yourself and let others help you.

Postpone important decisions
Making important and meaningful long-term decisions requires logical reasoning, a sense of objectivity and rational thought processes. You are unlikely to possess these skills while you are suffering from depression. Getting married or divorced, buying or selling a property, or changing jobs, are significant life decisions, which can also be stressful. It is best to defer these until you feel better. Before making them, you should discuss any intended plans or proposals with others who know you well and have a more objective view of your situation.

Continue to educate yourself about depression
I struggled for a long time to understand depression. I discovered that the better informed you are, the better choices you will make and the more confident you will be that you have made the right choices when it comes to your pathways to recovery and future wellbeing. Today, information is more readily available than ever. Go in search of it. It is there.

Keep asking questions, especially of your health professionals
At first, I attended appointments with doctors and psychologists without making any assessment of the value of the advice I was receiving and the direction I was taking. I asked some obvious questions like those discussed in Chapter One and often left the consultation with a blind acceptance of what they thought was right for me. In doing so, I was ignoring the vital role that I could play in directing the traffic towards addressing the things that I needed to make progress towards my recovery—not just listening to a diagnosis and advice about what had worked for others.

> *What will my journey look like? What is the best pathway for me? What assistance do I need to help me get to where I need to be? Who can provide that assistance? What type of therapy would suit me best? Is the proposed treatment plan right for me? Is this doctor, this psychologist or therapist best suited to assist me through my journey?* (I will talk about this more in Chapter Six.) *Who can I reach out to if it all falls apart on a Saturday night?*

These are some practical questions worth asking as you progress on your journey. Keep asking them of yourself and those assisting you, your Recovery Team. You should never stop. Your needs and the answers you seek may change over time. If one of your Recovery Team cannot provide a solution, seek it out, educate yourself. Information can be powerful. It can help you make choices that are right for you. That is the end goal.

Failed options

Success is just as much about failure as it is about achieving your goals. Without failure, there is nothing to learn. With that in mind, it is worth noting that I often failed in my attempts to pursue a practical recovery pathway or select the 'right' treatment options. The critical thing to remember is to take the learning derived from these failed options and use it as a foundation for making your future decisions. I have outlined some of my failed attempts. There were many more.

Alcohol and illicit drugs

As much as you try them, alcohol and illicit drugs will never take away the pain; they just keep prolonging it by worsening your symptoms and inhibiting your treatment. These things will inevitably lead to a collision that could damage your pathways to recovery, extend your journey with the illness or bring your life to an abrupt end. These facts are indisputable. Do not risk it.

Avoiding the excessive consumption of alcohol or use of illicit drugs will help you take control, to get into the driver's seat. Remember, you must always drive sober. That way, you avoid collisions and give yourself the best chance of getting to your destination.

Rushing recovery and risking relapse

Depression is a highly recurrent illness.[127] A significant part of sustained recovery from depression is, therefore, being able to avoid or cope with relapse risk factors.[128] Consequently, it is prudent not to rush recovery efforts, which can be an easy thing to say when, for example, you are not working and are experiencing financial and other pressures. The main point is that you take the time needed for you to recover from the illness. There is no right amount of time. It will take as long as it takes. Keep in mind that it is better to invest the time and effort in your recovery than it is to have to prolong these endeavours because of a recurrent episode brought about by an unreasonable expectation that you ought to have recovered sooner. The 'right' amount of time for you to improve your condition is the amount of time that it takes. It is as simple as that.

Other alternatives

Modern technology has also enhanced suicide prevention options through the availability of apps,[129] for example, which include features such as a safety plan, repositories for important photos, customisable self-help fields, built-in support options and sharing capability. These apps assist sufferers by promoting help-seeking behaviour, increasing access to support in times of crisis and overcoming barriers to treatment. The opportunity to share safety plans with supporters is a valuable tool, which, when combined with the inherent features of these apps, may prove vital to reducing suicide rates globally.

There is a myriad of alternative coping strategies and techniques to those that I have outlined in this chapter. Yoga, meditation, self-care techniques and natural therapies are some examples of approaches that may be equally effective in dealing with mental illness.[130] To these, I would add the option of anything else that works for you. Explore your available options, try alternative strategies and decide what works best for you. There is no one-size-fits-all approach. Effective coping strategies are unique to you, and your ownership of these is vital to recovery.

CHAPTER SIX: YOUR RECOVERY TEAM

Alone we can do so little; together we can do so much.
— HELEN KELLER

Your Recovery Team is vital to your successful recovery from mental illness. Your team comprises anyone that you feel can provide you with meaningful guidance, support and understanding throughout your journey. Doctors, psychiatrists, psychologists, therapists, family members and close friends are examples, but this list is not definitive. It also means that you should exclude from membership people who are not perceived by you to possess these qualities. The wrong team members can destabilise your recovery efforts and impact the effectiveness of other team members. Be prepared to make changes because your team is likely to evolve with time.

In this chapter, I will outline my experiences in selecting a Recovery Team, including choosing a doctor and therapist. In my case, I dealt with GPs and psychologists. I will, therefore, discuss this aspect of counselling and therapy in more detail. You could expect similar considerations to arise in terms of the selection process concerning other therapy providers, so the information presented in this chapter will remain of use in those contexts. In Chapter Seven, I will provide practical tips to carers and supporters to allow them to become more effective in their support roles.

Selecting your therapist

A critical member of your team will be your therapist. Not all therapists are the same. Some are more qualified than others. Some more experienced. Each plays a different role, provides varying levels of guidance and support, and may specialise in certain types of therapy or theoretical orientation.[131] There is no fail-proof method of selecting the 'right' therapist for you, and the professional that works well for someone else might not work as well for you.[132] There are, however, important factors to consider that are vital to therapeutic outcomes and may assist in your decision-making.

Who can be your therapist?

In Australia, people engaging in therapy generally consult with a psychiatrist, psychologist, psychotherapist, psychoanalyst, counsellor, social workers, and other specialist therapists.[133] There are important differences between a psychotherapist and a counsellor, as well as between a psychologist and psychiatrist.[134]

You may find, as I did, that you will employ the use of a counselling and therapy team comprising your GP and psychologist. A psychiatrist might enter the scene on occasions to assess the suitability of medications, provide medical opinions or to assist generally in your treatment. According to Grohol (2019), 'Emotional stress can be relieved temporarily through medications (and can be an important adjunct to psychotherapy), but they generally are not used as a "cure."'[135] Hence, he recommends avoiding seeking help from a psychiatrist only, for almost all mental disorders.

If you are unsure, consult your GP or access information and services provided by the relevant professional body[136] to determine which type of therapist may be the best choice in your circumstances.

How do I find a psychologist?

To find a psychologist or other therapist, ask your GP or another health professional. Committing to consult with your GP is the crucial first step to your recovery because it acknowledges you have a serious problem. Nowadays, most doctors in general practice will be adept at responding to the needs of patients suffering from the effects of mental illness,[137] and those with the relevant experience can also be competent counsellors. You may find, as I did, that your GP has an established network of referral partners, including psychologists and other therapists. Your GP is, therefore, a good source of referral.

Other options include consulting your local psychological association, relevant professional body,[138] a local university or college department of psychology, asking family and friends, and contacting your area's community mental health centre or local community support groups.

What to consider when making the choice

Finding the right therapist has been likened to app dating.[139] You hope it will be a good match, but sometimes you are left disappointed.[140] When you are disclosing your intensely personal emotional problems into the hands of a stranger, and paying them to help you, it is prudent to expect a connection, albeit professional.[141] Hence, the right match is critical.

It is essential to remember from the outset that therapy is not an easy process. If your treatment is comfortable, it might be a sign that you or your therapist is not working hard enough.[142]

Similarly, if you are not experiencing the outcomes that formed part of your treatment plan with the therapist, it may be time to change therapists.

Like many important relationships in life, finding the right therapist can take some experimentation.[143] You should be prepared to change as often as needed until you find the right fit, remembering that you must remain an active participant at all stages of therapy. I changed therapists twice during my journey and was fortunate to have found one on my third attempt that ticked all the relevant boxes. Other sufferers report having consulted with 'practically all of the psychiatrists'[144] in town before striking gold. The message here is that it doesn't matter how many times it takes to find the 'right' therapist for you because their role is vital to your recovery. It is also important to note that your therapist is not there to be your friend[145] but rather to facilitate your journey to recovery.

In my experience, there are necessarily three relevant factors to consider when making your initial choice and maintaining a meaningful professional relationship with your doctor and therapist, namely: trust (incorporating establishing a rapport or connection), experience and confidence in outcomes.

Most doctors, psychologists and therapists will have fulfilled the academic and professional requirements to entitle them to practise in their location. Once you establish their credentials and competence, your level of personal comfort with that doctor or psychologist, including establishing a good rapport, is critical.[146] Choose one with whom you feel comfortable and at ease.[147] This process may involve being very selective in terms of your preferences, for example, by expressing a preference for a practitioner who is male or female, young or old, gay or straight, ethnically diverse or otherwise. On my third attempt, I went in search of a male therapist about the same age as I was, with a family composition similar to mine, and comparative life experience outside of psychology. In my mind, I was more likely to connect with someone with these attributes. Fortunately, this proved to be true. This approach is perfectly acceptable[148] because the treatment should be all about you and your efforts to find the 'right' treatment in your circumstances. Unless you do so, you cannot expect to receive the full benefits of therapy.[149]

Trust must always exist in relationships with professional workers. In my view, there are two essential elements to this equation. You must first 'like' them. By that, I mean feel comfortable talking to them. Second, you need to trust them to listen without judgement and to offer considered and well-reasoned advice based on your individual needs. If you cannot, and you feel like you must lie to your doctor or therapist, or withhold important information, you are not going to get any real help.[150]

Some writers recommend seeking out 'therapists who have been practising in the field for at least a decade, longer when possible'[151] because it means they will be more likely to help you. I am not sure about the need for a minimum period of experience but agree that it is undoubtedly an important consideration. I would tend to prefer the quality of a therapist's expertise over tenure.

Grohol (2019) suggests determining the suitability of a therapist may result from a quasi-interview process that involves you asking questions of the therapist during your initial session and adjudging the responses to see whether the therapist will help you or not accordingly.[152] Another practical option is to arrange a time for an over-the-phone interview to get a sense of who they are before committing to an initial session.

The American Psychological Association (2020)[153] has formulated a list of questions that it considers are appropriate to ask of a prospective therapist. I have set these out below with some slight adaptations. Parts of the last one are location-specific, but these elements may be appropriately modified to suit the health care systems of other countries.

- Are you a licensed psychologist? How many years have you been practising psychology?
- I have been feeling (anxious, tense, depressed, etc.), and I'm having problems (with my job, my marriage, eating, sleeping, etc.). What experience do you have helping people with these types of issues?
- What are your areas of expertise?
- What kinds of treatments do you use, and have they been proven effective for dealing with my type of problem or issue?
- What are your fees? (Fees are usually based on a 45-minute to 50-minute session.) Do you have a sliding-scale fee[154] policy?
- What types of insurance do you accept? Will you accept direct billing to or payment from my insurance company? Are you affiliated with any managed care organisations? Do you accept Medicare[155] or Medicaid[156]?

At some point in therapy, you must also feel that going to your therapist is helping you. You need to be confident in the outcomes. If you do not feel relief from your emotional problems, you may not be getting the best treatment available. Look at these types of warning signs as reasons to think about choosing another therapist if you are already in therapy, or signs to look out for during your initial few sessions with a new therapist.[157]

Another consideration is the therapeutic approach adopted by the therapist.[158] Good Therapy Australia observes that 'there are many schools of thought in therapy, and the myriad of possibilities can be daunting.'[159] Discuss the relevant approaches with your GP and incorporate into your selection criteria the therapeutic approach most suited to your needs.

Finally, your therapist needs to be available. You should ensure the therapist is conveniently located. Also ask whether suitable appointment times are available to suit your needs. If you require flexible consultation alternatives, such as the use of teleconference or videoconference if you live in a remote location or cannot physically access the therapist's rooms for any reason, you should also ensure that these are viable.[160] There is no point engaging a therapist if you can never get in to see them when you need them most. In my experience, you may also expect to wait for an initial appointment with 'good' therapists. I waited several months but, in the end, it was worth it and better than wasting that time and money with another therapist that was not effective in responding to my needs.

What to expect in your first few therapy sessions

I had never been to a therapist before depression and anxiety. I had absolutely no idea what to expect, how I should behave, whether I should do the talking or what constituted good or bad therapy. I eventually found the answers to these mysteries. I will share these with you shortly.

Before I do, I want to outline what you might experience after you have selected your therapist and committed to attend your first few sessions. Remember that each therapist will have their own way of conducting sessions so your experience might be slightly different to those that I will describe.

At my first few sessions with the first of my therapists, I sat there like a stunned mullet. I had no clue about what to say or do. I went in there looking for the couch to lie down on like people do in the movies. When I only saw a chair, I was confused. I developed a new understanding of how my own clients must have felt when they came to see me about their legal and business problems. I really felt lost, alone and overwhelmed by the experience.

After a few introductory questions and answers, I was shocked that my therapist was asking me for advice about how she should approach legal issues concerning the lease of her premises and conduct of the landlord. This subject dominated our first few sessions. I'd had enough by the third one and decided to find another therapist.

I learned two things as a consequence. The first lesson was that I should always be prepared to speak up and be actively involved in my own therapy. The second was to look for warning signs that indicated the therapist might not be the right one for me and then to have no hesitation to change. I will talk about identifying these warning signs in the next section. Perhaps a third, less serious, lesson was that not all therapists have a place to lie down!

What I should have expected during these first few sessions were questions surrounding the reasons that I was seeking therapy, my personal history, present situation and my current symptoms.

In the initial session, you can expect a getting-to-know-each-other type of meeting. The first visit is likely to involve you completing a client intake form (or questionnaire) and some basic questions from the therapist so that he or she can get an idea about how to proceed with your therapy. This is also an opportunity for you to ask any questions of your therapist, or express concerns that you may have. You need to make sure it will be a good match.

In providing responses to the therapist's questions, you should be prepared to be open and honest about your feelings. You should also keep asking questions and come prepared for the next session of therapy. This is the best way to get the most out of it. Future visits will be more therapeutic in nature so you can expect more detailed questions from the therapist that begin to drill down on the specifics of your initial discussion as well as your prevailing progress. In the next few sessions, be prepared to thoroughly outline your personal and family history, your symptoms and their effects on you, your family, and your work. The subsequent sessions are when you are likely to find that most therapists will have supplies of tissue boxes.

Perhaps the most surprising and confronting lesson I learned from my participation in the first few sessions of 'good' therapy is that feelings and emotions can rise to the surface very quickly. It feels uncomfortable and unsettling, and renders you immensely vulnerable to someone you hardly know. I recall feeling raw and exposed in a way that I had never experienced before.

Reflecting on the effectiveness of the 'good' therapy that I received, I do not think it is possible to make any progress until you have been in this position. Until you have felt the way that I did in these sessions and later ones. Until you have wept uncontrollably like a baby, cried a river or two, and left a session feeling tired and exhausted. I used to have my sessions in the morning because it left me the afternoon to reflect. Most of the time, I fell asleep. Ultimately, when I awoke, I felt a lot better.

The tissues are usually free so my advice is to use them when you need them—it will make you feel a whole lot better and will mark the start of your journey to a meaningful, longer-lasting recovery.

The last thing you can always expect from your first few sessions and subsequent sessions with your therapist is confidentiality. This means that you can and should be as open and honest as you can be. There is no judgement in the process, only empathy from someone trained to listen and guide you. Let yourself go and give in to the experience and embrace its outcomes. Unless you do so, your journey with the illness will be a longer one.

Identifying warning signs

Just as critical to making the right choice of therapist for you is to be able to identify the warning signs which highlight that your therapeutic outcomes may not be in good hands.

Warning signs may be evident from your therapy sessions or within the approach adopted by your therapist. Shedler (2016) offers some practical advice about the warning signs to look for and the factors to consider in making your selection of therapist. He maintains that:

> *You steer clear of ideologues and experts-at-everything. You don't search far and wide for a therapist who specializes in people with exactly your problem because there are no other people with exactly your problem. When you meet, notice whether the therapist seems more interested in you or your diagnosis. Notice whether the therapist invites you to think together about what is the matter. Notice whether the two of you are able to develop a shared understanding of what is the matter that rings true, that was not already evident. The last*

part may take a few meetings, but the trajectory should be moving in that direction from the beginning. If all of these ingredients are there, you've probably found a good one.[161]

Other red flags that may warrant you moving on are if the therapist:

- does nothing more than nod his or her head and provide vague utterances of reassurance like 'I see' or ask questions that might seem dismissive (like the classic 'And how does that make you feel?') because this type of therapy proves ineffective, while a more positive and engaging therapist is better able to help a patient achieve optimal results;[162]
- continually watches the clock, makes you feel guilty for quitting, or threatens that you'll 'plunge into depression' if you stop going to therapy;[163]
- is talking more than you;[164]
- is interrupting you often;[165]
- exhibits any inappropriate behaviours (sexual or otherwise);[166] or
- has violated your confidentiality.[167]

Finding a therapeutic alliance

Research suggests that a strong relationship between a client and psychologist (known as the *therapeutic alliance*) is still one of the most important factors in determining the success of therapy.[168] According to Shedler (2016),[169] this alliance does not just mean that you feel a positive connection based on just *anything*. Instead, a therapeutic alliance is based on a shared purpose around the work you are there to do and has three elements, each of which must exist for there to be an effective alliance:

1. There is a connection.
2. There is mutual agreement about the purpose of therapy.
3. There is mutual agreement about the methods you will use in pursuit of this purpose.

The primary objective of your relationship with a therapist is a meaningful psychological change, not just a warm and supportive relationship.[170]

What is 'good' therapy?

One of the key ways to evaluate whether your therapy is 'good' and operative is to assess whether your initial sessions focus on developing a shared understanding of 'what is really the matter'[171] or the 'real' underlying issues, not just your symptoms. Development of a consensus that makes sense to both you and your therapist is a critical part of this process.[172] It could include the option of formulating a treatment plan with specific goals and objectives, including strategies that your therapist believes will help you reach those goals and the possibility of a time frame for getting there.[173]

According to Shedler (2016), the concept of 'what is really the matter' is not your depression or anxiety; instead, it is what is going on psychologically that is *causing* these difficulties. A shared understanding of what is the matter provides a focus for therapy—and effective treatment has a focus.[174] This process may commence in the first session and continue over subsequent sessions, evolving as treatment progresses. The basic premise is that there is no point 'doing' therapy unless both participants know what they are there to do.[175]

Good therapists will also demonstrate ethical boundaries by keeping the relationship professional, and limiting the personal information they share about themselves.[176] Staying awake and remaining alert throughout a session and not answering their phone or checking text messages[177] are also indicators of professionalism. You should never feel that your therapist is pushing his or her agenda or professional goals, like selling a book.[178] Like any competent professional, if your therapist is not capable of assisting you with your specific issue, you should expect to be referred by them to someone with the relevant expertise. You certainly do not want to be any therapist's first-time client for the problem you're experiencing. Knowledge and expertise regarding your issue are, therefore, critical competencies for a good therapist to possess.[179]

The other way to determine whether your therapy is 'good' is to assess if it is working. You can expect to experience a wide variety of emotions during therapy. You will know your therapy is working if you begin to feel a sense of relief, and a sense of hope because it can be a positive sign indicating that you are starting to explore your thoughts and behaviour.[180] It is important to remember that some goals require more time to reach than others, so adjust your expectations accordingly. You and your psychologist should decide at what point you may expect to begin to see progress.[181]

Here are some questions[182] you can ask yourself during and after sessions with your therapist to assist in your determination of whether you have found the 'right' psychologist for your mental health needs.

During the sessions

- Do you like and respect them, and are you feeling comfortable and understood?
- Are they asking adequate questions?
- Have you set clear goals and aims for when the therapy is over?
- Are you receiving feedback that makes you feel like you're on the right track?
- Have they outlined a treatment plan?

After the sessions

- Are you feeling hopeful and relieved?
- Do you feel empowered to make a change?

Evaluating other team members

The composition of your Recovery Team is likely to change over time as your needs change and develop during your recovery journey. Individual support people may become disillusioned, lose interest, no longer have the patience or time, or consider they can no longer provide the support you expected. There is nothing at all wrong with that. It is human nature. You must be prepared to continually evaluate your team to ensure that the people within it are providing an adequate level of support to enable you to proceed down your selected pathway to recovery. If they are not, you must act decisively in excluding them from the support team. While taking this action can be a hard thing to do, your recovery rests on it.

Most people will already have an established GP before a diagnosis. I did. In this scenario, the critical relationship elements with the GP may already be well-established. If so, the inclusion of the GP in your Recovery Team may be a foregone conclusion. Alternatively, you may feel as though your GP is more comfortable responding to your coughs, colds and physical symptoms and ailments than dealing with mental health issues. Another scenario, which I experienced, is that at some point you find that your GP is no longer providing you with the level of support in your journey that you expected or need. In these situations, you are likely to need to find a GP that can meet your ongoing mental health needs. Considerations about selecting a therapist could apply equally to your GP, even though your GP and therapist perform different support roles in your Recovery Team.

Perhaps the most difficult decision to make in this area relates to the possible inclusion of selected family members and friends in your Recovery Team. In my view, there is no hard and fast rule. You need to rely on your instincts. I think there is a logical argument justifying the inclusion in your group of only selected members of your immediate family (husband, wife and children). It might be possible that there can be too many cooks in your kitchen to render the support productive. You will indeed find out who your 'true' friends are in the process so, in many ways, that will resolve itself one way or another without substantial effort on your part. The bottom line is that you need support from people who will be useful contributors to your recovery journey.

To be a productive member of your Recovery Team, the adoption of some 'best practice'[183] principles by its participants is fundamental. These principles include having a non-judgemental attitude, promoting hope and recovery, being respectful of privacy and dignity and providing support when and where it is needed. Not all your family members or friends are likely to possess or be capable of demonstrating these qualities in the circumstances. Some may even appear to refuse to acknowledge your illness or its effects, let alone take the time to understand it or assist by supporting your recovery. Once again, this is human nature. While it may be disappointing when it involves family, try not to be disheartened. Instead, restore your focus on identifying and retaining members in your Recovery Team that want to be there for you and are prepared to provide the level of support that you need and deserve.

CHAPTER SEVEN: PRACTICAL TIPS FOR CARERS AND SUPPORTERS

*Unless someone like you cares a whole awful lot,
nothing is going to get better. It's not.*
— DR SEUSS, THE LORAX

If you are the wife, husband, family member or other carer or supporter of a person with depression, I would like to now provide you with some tools to help equip you to become a productive contributor in your supporting role. Support like yours is vital, and you have a critical function to play in the recovery process.

Before you commit to doing so, you should understand that supporting someone suffering from anxiety and depression is not easy. It can be physically and emotionally challenging. At times, it may conflict with your employment, relationships, social life, physical or mental health. It is, therefore, imperative that you also invest the time to look after yourself while supporting others.

One of the most challenging issues to understand for carers and supporters is how to communicate their support for their friend or loved one as they are suffering from the impact of the symptoms of depression. You should never feel afraid to say, '*I am not sure what to say right now.*'[184] It is better to say that than to utter words that may do more harm than good.

Typing the words 'what not to say to someone with depression' or 'what to say to someone with depression' into a search engine like Google will reward you with a plethora of useful information. Your search will link you to sites containing warnings about the use of certain words and phrases to be avoided when you are speaking to someone with depression, and those words that are encouraged in the interests of providing meaningful support.[185] Many of these are sourced from feedback from sufferers and provide invaluable insight into the power of words for someone experiencing depression. In the words of Robin Williams' character, John Keating, in the movie *Dead Poets Society* (1989), 'No matter what anybody tells you, words and ideas can change the world.' For a carer or supporter, words can help build a connection, and communicate support in a way that is meaningful to someone suffering from anxiety or depression.

Platitudes do not cure depression

Most people offer advice or support to someone they care about with depression with only the best of intentions. If you do not understand the nature of depression and its impact, the words you use may not convey the message you want to send.[186] Platitudes do not cure depression.[187] Although often uttered unintentionally, they may be considered by a person with depression to be trivialising their illness[188] and can do more harm than good.[189]

From personal experience, I can attest to feeling attacked, isolated, misunderstood and deeply hurt by comments from people I thought were close to me while I was suffering from depression (particularly during major episodes) when they said things like:

> *Robert should just get over it and move on.*
> *If you can't handle the pressure, then do something else.*
> *Cheer up. It can't be that bad!*

In Chapter Two, I outlined some of the symptoms I was experiencing at various times throughout my journey. During severe episodes, I was debilitated. Thoughts of death were pervasive. I was at rock bottom. Imagine experiencing these symptoms and hearing these types of comments made by people you were expecting to be there to support you. It cuts deep, exacerbates symptoms, and sends you on a tumultuous ride into utter despair, misery and agony, way beyond where you were in the first place.

It goes without saying that language 'can have a big impact on how someone feels about their mental health condition or recovery process'.[190] It is, however, unfair to expect a carer or supporter to have to worry about saying the 'wrong' thing or having to obsess over their word choices needlessly. It is enough for them to state that they do not know what to say and assure the sufferer that they are there for them[191] because, amongst other things, depression can make a person feel isolated and alone. Sometimes, just being there can be all that is required to provide meaningful support.

Carers and supporters should educate themselves about what not to say and adjust their use of language to accommodate the needs of the person they are supporting. Try to use language that makes the sufferer feel empowered to seek support and brings with it hope that things will get better.[192] Empowerment can come from acknowledging someone's depression for what it is (not a phase) and giving them tacit permission to feel depressed (not 'but why should you be sad?').[193]

I have compiled a table of some of the most common language to avoid, and the reasons for it, to assist carers and supporters develop a general understanding of how these words are likely to be perceived by someone suffering from anxiety or depression. I hope you find it useful.

TABLE 1: WHAT NOT TO SAY

PHRASE: *I know exactly how you feel.*

PERSPECTIVE: Even if you have experienced depression, you still may not know how the sufferer feels because everyone is different and their experience with the illness unique. The other point is that no one knows exactly how anyone else feels. This phrase is not a helpful way to make someone feel understood when their depression has become overwhelming.[194]

PHRASE: *But you don't look depressed!*

PERSPECTIVE: The 'invisible' nature of mental illness can often mask its effects. The way someone presents to the outside world does not necessarily reflect how they are feeling. People with depression and anxiety will often go out of their way to 'put on a happy face' and hide how they feel from others. In reality, they are likely to be feeling embarrassed, confused, guilty, ashamed, or afraid of what could happen if people find out they are depressed.

This mindset can lead to fears about co-workers regarding them as incompetent, or people close to them ceasing to love or care for them. Even though they do not reflect reality, these feelings can be very intense and are characteristic of depression. It is, therefore, essential to look deeper in attempts to identify warning signs.

Just because someone with depression conceals it from others does not mean that they do not want to talk about how they are feeling. Undoubtedly, it takes courage to speak openly about the illness and the pain it causes. If you respond with doubt or disbelief, it may make the sufferer feel like talking about their depression is not safe and begin to question themselves and whether it is worthwhile seeking treatment.[195]

PHRASE: *Snap out of it.*
or
Get over it.

PERSPECTIVE: This is possibly one of the worst things to say to someone with depression. A sufferer has no way to turn depression on and off. Depression is an illness like any other physical illness, so the message conveyed by these words is not only impossible for the person with depression to comply with, it evidences a lack of compassion, empathy and understanding of the nature of the illness.

PHRASE:	*What do you have to be depressed about?* *or* *You have no reason to be depressed.*
PERSPECTIVE:	Reminding someone with depression about how lucky they are to live the way they do, or not to have to endure the pain and suffering of those less fortunate in the world, is not at all helpful to someone suffering from depression. While people may be worse off than the sufferer, it doesn't feel that way to someone who is depressed.[196] A likely response to these statements from someone with depression might be: 'You're right. So, there must be something wrong with me.'[197]

If the person is having persistent thoughts that the world would be better off without them and considering suicide as a real option for them to find that escape, these words can be a powerful endorsement of a perception that is not true.

These words can make a depressed person feel guilty, ashamed or like their feelings don't matter [198] in circumstances where they are likely to be already experiencing these emotions. Depression often has no specific reason, trigger or cause,[199] so asking questions or making statements of this kind and expecting a depressed person to acknowledge a contrary position is unfair and does nothing to assist them to recover from the illness.

Finally, it is not possible to argue someone out of depression. Instead, demonstrate your understanding and support.

PHRASE:	*Just have a drink and relax.*
PERSPECTIVE:	Alcohol is a depressant.[200] Hence, it is not advisable to encourage someone with depression to consume alcohol, nor is it the panacea or a cure from the effects of the illness.

PHRASE:	*Don't be so negative.* *Think happy thoughts.* *or* *Cheer up!*
PERSPECTIVE:	Depression would not exist and be so prevalent around the world if it were that simple. Implying that depression is a choice communicates a false assumption. There is no way for someone with depression to flick a switch to make it go away, nor do so with happy thoughts and perhaps a smile. It takes hard work, commitment, and strong support to recover from depression. This statement ignores that reality. It also oversimplifies the intense feelings of sadness (way beyond those experienced by everyone from time to time) that are associated with depression.

PHRASE:	*Everyone gets depressed sometimes.*
PERSPECTIVE:	While everyone may experience sadness, or have a bad day, not everyone will get depressed, so this statement is untrue. It is also dismissive of the illness and the likely impact it is having on the sufferer.

PHRASE:	*You just need to get out and do something* *or* *Why don't you go for a nice walk?*
PERSPECTIVE:	Depression keeps you from wanting to engage in everyday activities. Symptoms like fatigue, loss of energy or tiredness can make small tasks like going for a short walk seem challenging or require more effort than usual. You can show support by offering to take a walk, go to a movie, or do some other activity with them, perhaps initiating this by saying something like: *'I know you don't feel like going out, but let's go together.'*[201]

PHRASE:	*You are being really selfish.*
PERSPECTIVE:	Supporting someone with depression is not easy. It can be an emotional rollercoaster, which makes it lonely and unpleasant for you too. Young (2020) offers some sound advice and highlights the issue this way: *'What's hard is that in a relationship the emotional resources generally go straight to the person who is struggling the most so there might not be much left in the kitty for you. What's important to remember though is that the person with depression will already be giving themselves a hard time. Depression is a physical illness, not a choice. Let them know that you miss them. And don't stop loving them.'*[202]

PHRASE: *It's all in your head.*

PERSPECTIVE: Suggesting that depression is something of the imagination is neither constructive nor accurate.[203] While there may be a perception held by some people that someone can think themselves into and out of depression—that it can be miraculously wished away—the fact is that depression is a 'real medical condition'[204] not a fanciful creation that can be turned on at night-time before bed or in the morning before breakfast.

Try saying instead, '*I know depression is real and that it is causing you to feel this way.*' In this way, you are acknowledging depression for what it is—an illness, not something imagined. In doing so, you are allowing the sufferer to feel supported through your acceptance of the facts and giving recognition to the way they are feeling in response to the illness.

PHRASE: *You just need to be better at dealing with it.*
or
Try harder.

PERSPECTIVE: There is no one-size-fits-all way of dealing with depression. Everyone responds to it in their own way. Someone with depression will be dealing with it every day. No breaks, no vacations. Just relentless responses to the illness that engulfs them in a persistent daily struggle to find some way of dealing with its effects. To suggest that a depressed person needs to get better at dealing with their illness is to foster 'another round of self-doubt, self-criticism and hopelessness. So just don't.'[205] It is demoralising and 'may make a person with depression feel their situation is hopeless.'[206]

PHRASE: *Hang in there. It will pass.*

PERSPECTIVE: Someone experiencing depression is likely to have been feeling that way for some time with no substantive improvement in their condition. That is why they need your help. A statement like this one is unhelpful because it implies that the illness will come and go like a weather storm, or a phase or fad of some kind. This is not true.

PHRASE: *It can't be that bad.*
or
It could be worse.
or
You think you have it bad...

PERSPECTIVE: Drawing comparisons of pain ignores the fact that emotional and physical suffering is not only subjective but relative.[207] It also diminishes their experience and can make them feel like you are not really listening to what they are telling you. This reduces your effectiveness as a member of the Recovery Team. People with depression also lack the internal resources needed to cope with stress in an effective and healthy way.[208] This can make seemingly minor annoyances or trivial inconveniences feel like insurmountable obstacles to someone with depression.[209]

No magic words

Unfortunately, there are no magic words to help a person struggling with depression feel better. It does, however, help to acknowledge your understanding that depression is an illness—not a phase or some sort of attention-seeking behaviour.[210]

It is common for supporters to feel unsure about how to talk to people with depression or anxiety or to worry about saying the wrong thing.[211] Statements that make a sufferer feel listened to, understand and hopeful that things can improve are vital to adequate support. It is important to observe that any statement of support offered must be intentional, expressed as truth and with meaning, and be accompanied by an intention to follow through on any promise or commitment made to the sufferer. An unkept promise can lead to the person supported feeling even more isolated, abandoned and alone than their symptoms are already making them feel.

Here is a table that I have composed using information available from several sources and my experience. It not a complete list of all the words and phrases that may work, but it will be a useful guide to some that do.

TABLE 2: WHAT TO SAY

PHRASE:	*I'm here for you.* or *There's nothing you can say to me that will send me away from you.*
PERSPECTIVE:	Depression and anxiety can make people feel very isolated and alone, which can be overwhelming.[212] Knowing that someone is there to help unconditionally makes it easier to reach out[213] and can help a depressed person deal with the unwarranted shame and stigma around depression.[214] It is vital to keep that promise and follow up with offers to help in small ways such as suggesting to go for a walk together, get prescriptions filled or selecting a program or movie to watch together on a designated weeknight.[215] These words and actions can help someone suffering feel supported.
PHRASE:	*I care.* or *I care about you, and it seems like you're really struggling. Would you be open to talking to a doctor or counsellor about what you're going through?*
PERSPECTIVE:	Feeling like the entire universe is against you is common with depression. These two simple words can, therefore, mean a great deal to someone in this mindset. Actions like gesturing for a hug or a light touch of a person's hand can convey the same message.[216]

Reaching out to let the sufferer know that they matter to you is a crucial part of this important message of support.[217]

PHRASE: *How can I help?*
or
What can I do to help? Just tell me how.

PERSPECTIVE: Depression imposes considerable weight on the sufferer, both physically and mentally,[218] so there are likely to be a significant number of things that you could do to ease the burden. You might think that dropping off meals or picking up groceries is the best way to help but the sufferer may prefer other means.[219] They may also 'be reluctant to accept your offer for fear of becoming a burden on you, so make it clear that you don't mind and want to help in the same way you know they would for you in a similar situation.'[220] It is, therefore, essential to make suggestions and listen intently to what the sufferer needs.

Depression can also make a person so tired and feel so down that someone suffering from it may not even know what kind of help to ask for in the circumstances.

Schimelpfening (2020) suggests to 'be prepared with a few specific suggestions, which may include:

- Could you use some help with housework or grocery shopping?
- Would you like some company for a while?
- Would you like me to drive you to your doctor appointments?'[221]

Asking how you can help shows that you are willing to help in a way that suits them best even if it is just small tasks or daily household chores like the laundry, cleaning and washing the dishes. These might seem insignificant but doing them affords the sufferer more time to focus on recovery and treatment goals.[222] The help needed may change over time throughout their recovery, so be prepared to be flexible.[223]

NOTATIONS: Some writers consider that it is unlikely that you will get a response to these questions from someone with depression.[224] I tend to agree and highly recommend the suggested ways of overcoming the general nature of these questions (set out below).

Schimelpfening (2020)[225] observes that 'being specific in regard to both the time and activity can be helpful.'

For example, instead of saying, *'Is there anything I can do for you?'* perhaps ask: *'Could I come over on Saturday morning and do some yard work for you?'*

Because depression can make things seem pointless and overwhelming, Young (2020)[226] suggests 'narrowing down your offer' vis-à-vis the time and the task can yield a starting point.

Narrowing the timeframe might look something like this: *'I'll meet you after your session/therapy/doctor's appointment if you want',* while the task could be restricted by questions analogous to: *'What can I do to help with the kids?' 'I've made a curry. There's heaps. Can I bring some over for you? Just throw it in the freezer if you want.'*[227]

PHRASE: *Say nothing at all.*

PERSPECTIVE: Sometimes just showing up and being there is one of the best things you can do for someone suffering from anxiety or depression.[228] Tacit support can be powerful and establish a connection.

PHRASE: *I can see this is a really hard time for you.*

PERSPECTIVE: This phrase provides acknowledgement that the effects of anxiety or depression are tangible and real for the person suffering. Validating the experience in this way 'is one of the most helpful things you can say.'[229]

PHRASE: *This is not your fault.*

PERSPECTIVE: People suffering from depression often have intense feelings of guilt for everything in their lives (even though this is not appropriate) and place blame upon themselves to the point that, in their minds at least, it starts to become factually based and overwhelming. For them, it feels like they did something to cause the illness. Communicating that the disease is not the fault of the sufferer alleviates the burden of these feelings of guilt and blame by acknowledging that anxiety and depression are a 'disease, not a choice'.[230] It also serves as a reminder to them that they can't just 'snap out of it' simply because it is common for mental health issues to be perceived (wrongly) as easy to fix on the surface. It's not an easy fix, and it's not their fault.[231]

PHRASE:	*I'm not sure what to do, but I am sure we can figure it out together.*
PERSPECTIVE:	Communicating that you do not know the answers but are willing to work together with the sufferer to find them is a strong statement of support. This statement can translate to: '*I'm not going to leave you or abandon you. We're in this together. You're not alone in this.*'
	These words provide assurance that the person is not alone, which may alleviate feelings of isolation common amongst sufferers.

PHRASE:	*I know it doesn't feel like it now, but there is hope that things can get better.* or *This isn't an ending. You can beat this.*
PERSPECTIVE:	Depression destroys hope. Hope is essential to recovery from anxiety and depression. Introducing the prospect of restoring hope and reminding a sufferer these illnesses are 'treatable, and with the right support, most people recover'[232] responds to the feelings of hopelessness and despair that become a staple of everyday life for someone that is depressed. It is, therefore, a powerful message to convey in sentiment and action.

PHRASE:	*Have you thought about seeing your doctor or calling support agencies? There is support available.* or *Asking for help is a sign of strength. Have you talked to your doctor about this?*

or
Depression is a real health issue that can be treated. What steps can you take to talk to a doctor or therapist about how you're feeling?

PERSPECTIVE: Available treatments for depression (such as therapy, medication, self-help, support groups, and exercise) are an essential part of the recovery process[233] but sufferers 'often feel ashamed of their condition or pessimistic about whether treatment will actually help.'[234]

Letting someone with anxiety or depression know that support is readily available and a necessary part of their recovery journey reinforces that they are not alone.

A Recovery Team should comprise professionals like doctors and therapists, family, and friends. Highlighting the importance of seeking professional support can encourage the sufferer to take the critical first step towards their recovery.

Combining this with an offer to drive them to appointments, for example, can ease the perceived burden of seeking help and remove it as a possible barrier to treatment.

....

PHRASE: *Take as long as you need.*

PERSPECTIVE: Depression can make everyday tasks like taking a shower, personal grooming, brushing your teeth or cooking feel overwhelming, especially during major (or severe) episodes. Thomas (2020) observes that 'many people with depression feel their mood lifts towards the end of the day, so allowing them extra time to do these tasks is a good plan.'[235] Recovery also takes the time it needs. Communicating that there is no requirement to rush the recovery process provides the sufferer with the opportunity to focus exclusively on their recovery from the illness without the worry of false or unreasonable expectations about timing.

PHRASE: *Depression is a real thing.*

PERSPECTIVE: People who are depressed are likely to feel like there is something wrong with them. By letting them know that you understand depression is an illness, you are reinforcing the notion that it didn't happen because there is something wrong with them,[236] that everyone is vulnerable to it and 'they were completely fine until depression happened'.[237]

Reaffirming that you are not going anywhere because one day it could be you[238] can also be a sound approach. It lets a sufferer know that they are not alone and gives them 'permission' (that is, lets them know it's okay) to feel depressed, which can be empowering to a person with depression.[239]

PHRASE: *You don't need to do anything that makes you feel uncomfortable.*

PERSPECTIVE: Feeling compelled to do something, like attend a function or social event, under obligation to 'put on a happy face' can be incredibly upsetting for someone with anxiety or depression. A sufferer is likely to be extremely stressed by the prospect that someone will publicly highlight their illness in some way, which can make them feel ashamed, embarrassed, and isolated. Thomas (2020) observes: 'Knowing that these events may be avoided for the time being can help a person feel relaxed and allow them the time to focus on their own health.'[240]

PHRASE: *Explain it to me. I want to understand.*

PERSPECTIVE: While depression affects people differently, the more you invest the time to understand it, the better. Showing your interest can translate quickly to a feeling of support. As Young (2020) explains: 'In the same way that you don't have to have a broken arm to know that it hurts, you don't have to have had depression to be an incredible support.'[241]

PHRASE: *You're a good person.*

PERSPECTIVE: Guilt can be a familiar feeling with depression and can be a trigger, as well as a symptom.[242] Someone with depression is likely to have intense feelings of being a bad person because they were too sick to go to work, attend a social function or family event (like a birthday, wedding or funeral) even when this is not true. As Thomas (2020) puts it: 'You wouldn't judge someone for missing an event due to physical illness, so why would you think someone was a bad person for being mentally unwell?'[243]

PHRASE: *I'd like to go with you.*

PERSPECTIVE: Depression can cause fatigue, feelings of worthlessness, guilt, and difficulty concentrating,[244] which interfere with routine aspects of daily life. People suffering from depression can find keeping a daily routine overwhelming. This can yield a reluctance on the part of the sufferer to make appointments with doctors, pick up medications, exercise or complete other aspects of treatment,[245] and can consequently become a barrier to seeking treatment. A sufferer can also feel like a burden to those supporting them.

Hurley (2018) observes that making an offer to help by driving them to 'appointments and assisting with other treatment goals lessens the feeling of being a burden and opens the door to communication.'[246]

PHRASE: *Do you feel like talking about it? It can be just between you and me, no one else.*
or
Do you want to talk about it? I'm here when you're ready.
or
I'm here for you. Whenever you want to talk, I'll listen—I'm just a call or a text away.[247]

PERSPECTIVE: Someone with depression is likely to have a lot of negative emotions bottled up inside them. Providing an opportunity for them to talk about these when it suits them may relieve some of the pressure of repressed feelings. Just having someone there who is prepared to sympathetically listen while the sufferer talks about what is bothering them can mean the world of difference. Be careful not to interrupt or allow the conversation to be taken over by your well-meaning advice.[248] It is also important to understand that a sufferer may not take you up on the offer straight away. It might be some time later that they do, so be prepared for that possibility.

You are really offering to listen more than anything else, so do so attentively because often people who are depressed just want an opportunity to talk. It is comforting to them to know that someone is prepared to listen, and this helps them feel supported.

By indicating that your conversations will remain confidential (unless they are at risk of hurting themselves), you are communicating respect for their privacy. You are also acknowledging that often people with depression feel ashamed of their illness and embarrassed or uncomfortable about seeking treatment while engendering trust in your relationship, which is vital to be a productive member of the Recovery Team.

PHRASE: *You mean a lot to other people and me.*

PERSPECTIVE: It is common for someone with depression to feel that their life does not matter, and no one would even care or miss them if they were gone.[249] Sincerely telling a sufferer about all the ways that they matter to you and others can help them realise they have value and worth[250] and thereby repress the feelings of worthlessness that are likely to have been pervasive in their day-to-day thinking.

PHRASE:	*You are not weak or defective. You're just sick and need to get better.*
PERSPECTIVE:	People with depression may feel like they are weak, that there is something wrong with them, or that they deserved to 'get' it. Assuring them that depression is an illness, and not payback for anything that they have done, reminds a sufferer that they are sick and just need to focus on getting better. Often people with depression will recover from the illness much stronger than they ever thought they were. If the person you are supporting has overcome a significant hurdle before being diagnosed with depression, this is a good reminder that they can do so again.
PHRASE:	*Do you feel like doing something together to help take your mind off things?*
PERSPECTIVE:	Talking to someone about how they feel all the time can sometimes be a distraction from other worthwhile activities. According to Beyond Blue (2020): 'Doing an activity you both enjoy can help people with anxiety and depression change the focus of their negative thinking and offer a sense of hope for the future.'[251]
PHRASE:	*Do you want some space?*
PERSPECTIVE:	Despite the common feelings of isolation during episodes of depression, time alone for

a sufferer can help them to digest how they are feeling, recharge their batteries and refocus on their treatment options.[252]

PHRASE: *I love you.*

PERSPECTIVE: Feeling alone, upset and helpless is common for depression sufferers and can be debilitating. While it may not be possible for you to have all the answers or know what to say or do all the time, just uttering these words can let someone with depression know that they have your support no matter what they are going through.[253]

PHRASE: *I have noticed that you seem to be doing better lately. Is that how it feels for you?*
or
Point out when you see a glimpse of their pre-depressed self. [254]

PERSPECTIVE: Only make this statement if you have observed positive changes that can be challenging to detect in someone with depression, particularly if they are small and gradual.[255]

According to Beyond Blue (2020): 'Gently pointing out your observations can help them feel like things might just be improving.'[256]

If you catch a glimpse of what the person was like before depression, Young (2020) recommends pointing it out every time as a reminder of life without it.[257] This is good advice.

PHRASE:	*I'm sorry if I said the wrong thing. Can we start again?*
PERSPECTIVE:	Depression is a complex subject. Talking through it is a challenging experience. It can be messy, emotional, and unpredictable, and serve to highlight the frailty inherent in human suffering at its worst. The critical part of having conversations with someone with depression is that it supports them and helps them recover.
	You should never beat yourself up if you say the wrong thing, or offence is taken to something you say. Just apologise. Explain that you weren't sure what to say, or that you didn't understand. Schimelpfening (2020) observes that an 'apology can help someone begin feeling better if your words haven't been helpful in the past.'[258] Being a good listener is often more important.

Even if it was possible to always say the 'right' things to someone with depression, it is still likely that your well-intended words of support will lead to them becoming angry or upset with you. That is the nature of depression. Throughout the journey, there will also be occasions when the person you are supporting will bite the hand that is feeding them by lashing out; the closest support person becomes the target. People with depression are hurting deeply inside. They are grappling with the reasons why and may never find them all, which can be incredibly frustrating. Venting their anger is often the only way of relieving this built-up tension. If this happens, try not to take it personally. Stay calm, give them space if they need it and continue to do what you can to support them in whatever way they will allow.

Finally, the risk of suicide is high in those living with depression.[259] Regardless of what you say or what you do to help someone experiencing depression, a sufferer may still experience suicidal thoughts and feelings.[260] Be on the lookout for warning signs and know when to seek help.

Warning signs

While supportive questions and actions are essential, often it is the careful listening and observation skills that become vital to the overall effectiveness of your support. A depressed person may not respond to the question *'Are you OK?'* by saying *'Actually, I'm not'.* Watching for signs that things might escalate can, therefore, be equally as important as learning what, and what not, to say to someone with depression.

The fact is that if you care for, or provide support to, someone with depression, there is a high risk that they will at some point think about suicide, particularly if they are suffering from severe depression.[261] The words and actions of someone contemplating suicide can provide clues that they are at risk of hurting themselves. Asking someone if they have suicidal thoughts will not give them the idea of suicide. This is a myth.[262] You should ask questions and gather facts to help someone who is depressed because the more people are willing to talk with a friend or family member about suicidal thoughts, the more likely they can help them take positive steps towards healing.[263]

It can be challenging to understand why someone has reached the point where they are considering ending their life. Suicide may be viewed by sufferers as a way to end the intense emotional pain they experience. Depression steals hope. When that is lost, everything in your life can feel hopeless. To some people, suicide seems like it is the only option because they lack any hope for the future. The focus of recovery pathways, therefore, must always be the restoration of hope.

While there is a strong relationship between mental health and suicide, and the risk is serious, it is essential to remember that most people with mental health conditions do not attempt or commit suicide.[264]

This may sound contradictory to the earlier observation that the risk of suicide is high in those living with depression but let me explain.

On the one hand, as you may recall from the discussion in Chapter One, someone with depression is twenty times more likely to die from suicide than someone without it.[265] Further, depression has been found to play a role in more than one-half of all suicide attempts.[266] Consequently, the risk of suicide is higher if you have depression, but it does not necessarily correlate that someone with it will attempt or commit suicide. Just because there is a higher chance of something happening does not necessarily mean that it will. Nonetheless, the risks are well-documented in research and should never be ignored.

Conversely, the incidence (or actual reported cases) of suicide in people with a mental illness of any kind, not just depression, is consistent with the general observation that most people will not commit suicide. This can also be explained by the numbers. In 2017, there were 972 million people around the world (or 10.7 per cent of the population) suffering from mental illness (including depression, anxiety, bipolar, drug, alcohol, eating and various other mental disorders).[267] The suicide rate among those collectively suffering from these mental disorders in the same period was 12.5 per cent,[268] meaning that the overall risk of suicide, generally, was substantially lower than for depression alone.

Knowing the risk factors (conditions associated with increased risk of suicide)[269] and warning signs of suicide is the best way to help prevent it.[270] Suicide is a complex topic requiring more detailed consideration. Educating yourself about the various risk factors and warning signs is imperative to maximising the effectiveness of your support in this area. To get you started, I will now provide a brief overview of these. It is not exhaustive.

Risk factors are categorised in a variety of ways.[271] Broadly, the most common risk areas relate to a person's health, environment, and history. Warning signs stem from the things someone says, their mood and behaviour.[272] Though it may be easier to recognise situations and times when suicide is more common, understanding how someone is feeling can be more difficult.[273]

Depression is not the only health risk factor for suicide. Other factors associated with an increased risk of suicide include other mental health conditions and disorders such as anxiety, substance abuse problems and personality traits of aggression, mood changes and poor relationships, and severe physical health conditions, including pain.[274]

A person's environment can also influence the risk of suicide. Some examples are prolonged stress, exposure to harassment, bullying, death or terminal illness of a relative or friend, another person's suicide, divorce, separation, or the breakup of a relationship, loss of a job, home, money, status, self-esteem, or personal security, access to firearms and drugs.[275]

Similarly, historical factors are also relevant. Prior suicide attempts, a family history of suicide, childhood abuse, neglect or trauma are associated indicators.[276]

The timing of certain life events can also make people more prone to suicidal feelings. Events such as anniversaries and holidays, the commencement of treatment with antidepressant medication, the diagnosis of a significant illness,[277] significant life changes (such as retirement) that lead to a loss of independence,[278] and court or disciplinary proceedings.[279]

While not everyone who suffers from one or more of the above conditions or situations will become suicidal, there is an elevated risk that people who do so will go on to experience changes in personality and behaviour that may increase the risk of suicide.[280]

Some of the emotional and behavioural changes that may increase the chance that a person may try to take their life include:

- talking about killing themselves, feeling hopeless, having no reason to live, being a burden to others, feeling trapped or experiencing unbearable pain;[281]
- increased use of alcohol or drugs, social withdrawal (or perhaps joining a group with different standards to those of the person's family), isolating from friends and family, looking for ways to end their lives (such as searching online for methods), changes in sleeping or eating habits (in either direction: suddenly sleeping or overeating, or sleeping or eating poorly), fatigue, giving away prized possessions, declining performance in school or work, feeling rage or uncontrollable anger or seeking revenge, inappropriate goodbyes or unexpected visits to friends and family members, especially combined with saying goodbye as if they won't be seen again;[282] and
- signs relating to mood such as depression, anxiety, loss of interest, irritability, humiliation and shame, agitation and anger, relief or sudden improvement.[283]

It may sound unusual to suggest that a sudden improvement in someone's condition could be a warning sign. Surely, it demonstrates that someone suffering from depression is getting better and may no longer be at risk? Not really.

Depression is not something that can be readily controlled with immediate precision. It can't be turned on and off at will. Improvements are usually gradual not sudden. Sudden improvement could indicate that the sufferer is attempting to mask how they are actually feeling and feigning an improvement in their condition to avoid close scrutiny by others. Abrupt improvements without a linked cause are also likely to be inconsistent with their mood in the time immediately preceding such an observation and thereby cause for alarm.

Alternatively, a sudden improvement in condition could indicate that the person has decided to end their life, engendering a sense of relief that a "solution" has been found.

Once again, not all people who experience these changes will become suicidal, but the risk for it is higher.[284] Some who experience such changes will go on to exhibit suicidal behaviours, marking the final step in the journey to suicide.

A note about warning signs

While most people who attempt suicide do show some sort of warning signs, there are also those people who, because of social stigma or a desire to not appear weak, will successfully hide what they are feeling[285] and may hide the effects of any associated changes. If the person exhibits even a few of the above features in any of the categories, they need to be taken seriously.[286]

However, failing to recognise the warning signs in these situations is not a source of blame. Doing the most you can do with the information you have is invariably the only option you have to lend support.

Prevention tips

There are things you can do to support someone with the urge to suicide. Encourage them to seek help from a mental health professional. If they refuse, be persistent. If they appear to be in immediate danger of hurting themselves, do not leave them alone, remove any possible means that they can use to hurt themselves, and get them to an emergency room as soon as possible.[287] In the longer term, support will hinge on your ongoing presence in their life, encouraging them towards actions that keep them in life.[288]

The Australian Institute of Professional Counsellors has developed some useful tips to help, including some practical questions for supporters to ask in assessing the risk posed to the supported person and statements to make that provide confirmation of your support in these circumstances.[289] Without seeking to diminish the intrinsic value of the publication, the essential guidelines may be summarised in point form as follows:

- Take the situation—and the person—seriously.
- Be pro-active: start 'The Conversation' about suicide.
- Assess their risk level.
- Be prepared to act quickly in a crisis.
- No secrets—do not agree to keep suicidal plans a secret!
- Urge professional help.
- Make a safety plan.[290]
- Plan to follow up on their treatment.

- Assure the person of your support over the long haul; offer it proactively.
- Encourage a healthy lifestyle.

Encouraging and even facilitating the use of suicide prevention apps, like those I mention in Chapter Five, is a powerful mechanism specifically designed to assist in the practical prevention of suicide. The sharing of safety plans with supporters is an invaluable feature of these apps.

Self-care for the supporter

Offering support to someone with depression, who may or may not be suicidal, can generate a broad range of feelings. Throughout the journey, you are likely to find it confronting, confusing, stressful, and even overwhelming. As with any other time of stress, you must look after yourself emotionally and physically. It is about finding the right balance for you—balancing how much you can offer the supported person while also looking after your own needs.[291] There are ways you can achieve this balance to deal with the stresses of helping someone with depression or anxiety. For example, staying connected with your friends and family, taking regular breaks, setting boundaries regarding the nature or type of support you will provide, asking other people for help, making time for yourself and maintaining a healthy lifestyle. It is often a thankless task, but I hope that if you are a member of the Recovery Team for someone you care about, it becomes a rewarding experience.

For your support, you deserve all the accolades the world can offer.

ROBERT NICHOLLS

CHAPTER EIGHT: BEYOND DARKNESS

*It's no use going back to yesterday because
I was a different person then.*
— LEWIS CARROLL, ALICE'S ADVENTURES IN
WONDERLAND

Depression is a journey. Like any trip, it will have obstacles and setbacks. There are also many ways to get to your destination. You can choose to be the driver or a passenger. Taking the wheel is the only way to guarantee that you will travel in the right direction, along the pathways you select to arrive at your recovery destination. You must dictate the route. You decide.

Before you take the keys, you must be prepared to go the distance even if there are pit stops you must make along the way. Consulting with your GP is likely to be the first stop on your journey to recovery. Commit to seeking help; everyone needs it. Regularly evaluating your treatment and its delivery is also imperative. Exploring all your options is essential. It is also necessary to accept that treatment involves pain; perhaps, lots of pain. Without it, there will be no benefit and your suffering will be prolonged. Take the time to heal and do not rush it.

You will become a more robust, better person at the end of your journey, but you must embrace the inevitable change that will accompany your passage beyond the darkness. Self-discovery can be immensely empowering in your battle because it will make you stronger. Learn to invest in the process by educating yourself and keep asking questions until you have the information you need to fuel your recovery.

Recognise the barriers to your treatment. Keep trying to overcome these barriers by focusing only on those that are within your power to surmount. Use the coping strategies that I have outlined or develop and implement other strategies that work for you. Learn from my mistakes and try to avoid the options that are doomed to fail, like rushing your recovery or using alcohol and drugs as a substitute for proper treatment.

Be flexible in your recovery plan because there is no one-size-fits-all approach. Your pathways are likely to change as your journey progresses. Adapting to these changes helps you to choose the recovery pathways that are 'right' for you. Keep assessing what this means.

Think of your supporters as road maps. They are there to help guide you. Working together with your supporters will help restore hope. It may be lost, but it is not gone altogether. At a stage in your journey, you are likely to reach the very lowest point in your existence on this planet. You will know when you get there. While it may sound unduly optimistic, it is only from this point, your lowest ever in life, that you can start to recover.

From there, it is critical that you commit yourself to improving day by day, breaking the issues down into pieces and working on them before moving on to the next one.

From there, you will find only improvement, and unparalleled opportunities to overcome the illness and assess your future options for life, work, and everything else.

From there, you begin your journey of rediscovering hope.

Hope definitely exists. Look for the signs. Sometimes they can be unpredictable and present at times when you may least expect it. Laugh when you can. Remind yourself of all the good things about the person you once were and focus on the stronger, better person you will have an opportunity to become.

Some people will find hope in religion or even perhaps visits to spiritual leaders in exotic locations. Others in philanthropy, an investment of their time and resources in the preservation of the planet, conservation of wildlife or even mental health advocacy.

You will find hope in your own way. It doesn't matter where you find it, just that you do. Like 'the truth' in the American science-fiction drama TV series, *The X-Files*, hope 'is out there'! It might only come to you in the final episode of your recovery pathway, but it will return.

Remember that you are not weak. You never deserved to have depression or anxiety. No one does. It is not payback for anything that you have done. You are just sick. You need to focus on getting better. That journey will take time and will not be an easy one. But it is a necessary one because the world is a much better place with you in it. Put the black dog back on its leash. Keep fighting as you have done in your life before depression. Make sure you are the last one standing. Finding hope again will starve depression. Keep trying your best not to feed it, one day and one issue at a time.

Remind yourself before you go to bed to wake up tomorrow, and tell yourself every day that you will be surviving the darkness.

What did you think?

First of all, thank you for purchasing *Surviving the Darkness*. I know you had the option of selecting any number of books to read, but you picked this book and for that I am extremely grateful.

One of the best ways for independent authors like me to get exposure for my book is to receive as many honest, thoughtful reviews as possible.

I crave to know what you thought about my first book and if it provided the intended practical assistance to you or someone you know. I sincerely hope so.

Please visit the place from which you purchased my book and leave a review. I appreciate your feedback, and so might others in need of help. Thanks in advance.

Stay strong and keep surviving the darkness.

Robert Nicholls

Acknowledgments

I had always wanted to write a book but never thought that it would take me this long or be on this topic. It taught me that you are never too old to be naïve and to learn.

For many reasons, it was not an easy book to write. It is, after all, my first book. It is also about a subject that I still find difficult to talk about, especially when it comes to relating my own experiences with depression and anxiety and, in doing so, expose my shortcomings for the whole world to read about and pass comment on. But that is where the self-pity must end because this was an important book to write.

For me, it was a cathartic experience. More importantly, it provided the opportunity to share with others the invaluable lessons that I have learned in discovering the pathways to recovery and, ultimately, in surviving the darkness. If this book saves just one life and, with that, a family eternal misery, then from my perspective, it has been well worth the adventure. I hope that it also contributes in its own small way to the erosion of the stigma that still unfairly attaches to people with depression and anxiety.

I would not have had the intestinal fortitude to write this book or to talk publicly about my experiences without a supportive network of immediate family, close personal friends, and health care professionals.

To ensure that I have the best chances of remaining married to my beautiful wife, Nadine, for another twenty-five years, or more, I need to firstly extend to her my heartfelt and sincere appreciation and gratitude for her unrelenting courage and support. She was the rock when my world and our lives collapsed without warning and kept our family going during the darkest of times.

To my children, Maddison and Ryan, I will always be grateful to you both for the depth of your understanding, love and devotion that you displayed while your dad was falling apart before you without any explanation. I am so proud of you both.

During my illness, I lost some friends. I also discovered my true friends. George Randolf once observed that 'Truly great friends are hard to find, difficult to leave, and impossible to forget.' I have been fortunate enough to have some truly great friends that I will never leave or forget. Thank you all for never thinking to judge me, giving me space when I needed it, dropping everything to come and be with me, and for your unconditional support when I craved it.

Good doctors and therapists can be difficult to find. I was fortunate enough to have them support and guide me through the journey. They made me understand that I had to be the driver of my recovery pathways and gave me the steering wheel to get me there. To my doctor, Scott, I know that looking after my health is a part of your job, but I remain grateful to you for the meaningful way that you always undertake it. To Mark, thanks for suggesting that I start writing something and convincing me that I had something to say, especially at times when I thought the vessel would always remain empty.

To all of you, thanks for ensuring that I survived the darkness.

Finally, I would like to express my gratitude to my editor, Daina Lindeman, at The Expert Editor for her impeccable attention to detail and significantly enhancing my writing efforts, and to Nada Backovic for designing the cover and the inside text of the book ensuring that it came to life and was the best it could possibly be.

ENDNOTES

CHAPTER ONE

1 For non-Australian readers, New South Wales is a state of Australia located on its eastern coast. It borders Queensland to the north, Victoria to the south, and South Australia to the west. Its coast borders the Coral and Tasman Seas to the east.

2 Newtown is a suburb in the inner west of Sydney. It is located approximately 4 kilometres (2.49 miles) from the Sydney CBD.

3 This was the term Winston Churchill purportedly used to describe his own depression: https://www.blackdoginstitute.org.au/.

4 For example, Munro, M. and Milne, R. (2020). Symptoms and causes of depression, and its diagnosis and management. *Nursing Times* [online], vol. 116, no. 4, pp. 18-22. Retrieved on 9 April 2020 from https://www.nursingtimes.net/roles/mental-health-nurses/symptoms-and-causes-of-depression-and-its-diagnosis-and-management-30-03-2020/: Dr Grohol, J. M. (2016). Depression, 27 January 2020. Retrieved on 23 April 2020 from https://psychcentral.com/depression/.

5 Misdiagnosis of depression is common: Bostwick, J.M. and Rackley, S. (2012). Recognizing mimics of depression: The '8 Ds'. *Current Psychiatry*, no. 11, pp. 31-36, because several illnesses have similar symptoms; for example, hyperthyroidism symptoms include low mood, reduced attention span and fatigue: Munro, M. and Milne, R. (2020). Symptoms and causes of depression, and its diagnosis and management. *Nursing Times* [online], vol. 116, no. 4, pp. 18-22. Retrieved on 9 April 2020 from https://www.nursingtimes.net/roles/mental-health-nurses/symptoms-and-causes-of-depression-and-its-diagnosis-and-management-30-03-2020/; and symptoms like weight change or insomnia, the most physical symptoms of depression, are not unique to depression. Such symptoms are common to many mental disorders: Dr Grohol, J.M. (2018). *The five symptoms of depression*, 8 July 2018. Retrieved on 17 April 2020 from https://psychcentral.com/blog/the-five-symptoms-of-depression/.

6 GBD (2017). Disease and injury incidence and prevalence collaborators. (2018) Global, regional and national incidence, prevalence, and years lived with disability for 354 diseases and injuries for 195 countries and

territories: A systematic analysis for the Global Burden of Disease Study 2017. *The Lancet*, vol. 392, no. 10159, pp. 1789-1858, 10 November 2018. doi: https://www.thelancet.com/journals/lancet/article/PIIS0140-6736(18)32279-7/fulltext.

7   The estimated world population in 2017 was approximately 7.6 billion: United Nations, Department of Economic and Social Affairs, Population Division (2017). World Population Prospects 2017 – Data Booklet (ST/ESA/SER.A/401). The population percentage was calculated by dividing the estimated world population by the number of people affected by depression, yielding about 3.5%.

8   Australia 4.66%; Canada 3.97%; New Zealand 4.12%; United Kingdom 4.12%; United States 4.81% and by way of an extreme example, Greenland 6.27%. Ritchie, H. and Roser, M. (2020). *'Mental health'*. Published online at OurWorldInData.org. Retrieved on 16 April 2020 from https://ourworldindata.org/mental-health [online resource]; Global Burden of Disease Collaborative Network. Global Burden of Disease Study 2017 (GBD 2017) Results. Seattle, United States: Institute for Health Metrics and Evaluation (IHME), 2018.

9   Ritchie, H. and Roser, M. (2020). *Mental health*. Published online at OurWorldInData.org. Retrieved on 16 April 2020 from https://ourworldindata.org/mental-health [online resource].

10 World Health Organization, *Depression fact sheet*, 30 January 2020. Retrieved on 9 April 2020 from https://www.who.int/news-room/fact-sheets/detail/depression.

11 Ibid.

12 Grohol, J.M. (2018). *The five symptoms of depression*, 8 July 2018. Retrieved on 11 May 2020 from https://psychcentral.com/blog/the-five-symptoms-of-depression/.

13 This was the term Winston Churchill purportedly used to describe his own depression, https://www.blackdoginstitute.org.au/.

14 Leonard Cohen referred to the illness as the 'darkness' in his song by the same name released in 2012.

15 Mark Mills, *He understood the darkness: On Leonard Cohen and depression*, Matter of Facts Blog, 12 November 2016. Retrieved on 17 April 2020 from https://matteroffactsblog.wordpress.com/2016/11/12/he-understood-the-darkness-on-leonard-cohen-and-depression/.

16 World Health Organization (2020). *Depression fact sheet*, 30 January 2020. Retrieved on 9 April 2020 from https://www.who.int/news-

room/fact-sheets/detail/depression; Munro, M. and Milne, R. (2020). Symptoms and causes of depression, and its diagnosis and management. *Nursing Times* [online], vol. 116, no. 4, pp. 18-22. Retrieved on 9 April 2020 from https://www.nursingtimes.net/roles/mental-health-nurses/symptoms-and-causes-of-depression-and-its-diagnosis-and-management-30-03-2020/; Bressert, S. PhD. *Depression Symptoms* (Major Depressive Disorder), 28 April 2020. Retrieved on 11 May 2020 from https://psychcentral.com/depression/depression-symptoms-major-depressive-disorder/.

17   Healthtact (2020). *What is depression*? 24 March 2020. Retrieved on 23 April 2020 from https://healthtact.com/what-is-depression.

18   Risks to mental health: An overview of vulnerabilities and risk factors (2012). World Health Organization; Ritchie, H. and Roser, M. (2020). Mental health. *Published online at OurWorldInData.org.* Retrieved on 16 April 2020 from https://ourworldindata.org/mental-health [online resource].

19   Munro, M. and Milne, R. (2020). Symptoms and causes of depression, and its diagnosis and management. *Nursing Times* [online], vol. 116, no. 4, pp.18-22. Retrieved on 9 April 2020 from https://www.nursingtimes.net/roles/mental-health-nurses/symptoms-and-causes-of-depression-and-its-diagnosis-and-management-30-03-2020/; Bressert, S. PhD. (2020). *Depression Symptoms* (Major Depressive Disorder). Retrieved on 11 May 2020 from Ritchie, H. and Roser, M. (2020). Mental health. *Published online at OurWorldInData.org.* Retrieved on 16 April 2020 from https://ourworldindata.org/mental-health [online resource].

20   Ritchie, H. and Roser, M. (2020). Mental health. *Published online at OurWorldInData.org.* Retrieved on 16 April 2020 from https://ourworldindata.org/mental-health [online resource]; Pietrangelo, A. (2018). *9 types of depression and how to recognize them*, 24 September 2018. Retrieved on 16 April 2020 from https://www.healthline.com/health/types-of-depression; Beyond Blue Ltd (2020). *Types of depression*. Retrieved on 16 April 2020 from https://www.beyondblue.org.au/the-facts/depression/types-of-depression.

21   Ritchie, H. and Roser, M. (2020). Mental health. *Published online at OurWorldInData.org.* Retrieved on 16 April 2020 from https://ourworldindata.org/mental-health [online resource], citing *The ICD-10 Classification of Mental and Behavioural Disorders Clinical descriptions and diagnostic guidelines*, World Health Organization. See also, for example, Malhi, G.S. et al. (2015). Royal Australian and New Zealand College of Psychiatrists clinical practice guidelines for mood

disorders, *Australian and New Zealand Journal of Psychiatry*, 2015, vol. 49, no. 12, pp. 1-185, and also in the American Psychiatric Association (2013). *Diagnostic and Statistical Manual of Mental Disorders*, 5th Edition.

22   Munro, M. and Milne, R. (2020). Symptoms and causes of depression, and its diagnosis and management. *Nursing Times* [online], vol. 116, no. 4, pp. 18-22. Retrieved on 9 April 2020 from https://www.nursingtimes.net/roles/mental-health-nurses/symptoms-and-causes-of-depression-and-its-diagnosis-and-management-30-03-2020/; Bressert, S. PhD. (2020). *Depression symptoms* (Major Depressive Disorder), 28 April 2020. Retrieved on 11 May 2020 from https://psychcentral.com/depression/depression-symptoms-major-depressive-disorder/.

23   Ritchie, H. and Roser, M. (2020). Mental health. *Published online at OurWorldInData.org.* Retrieved on 16 April 2020 from https://ourworldindata.org/mental-health [online resource].

24   The World Health Organisation's (WHO) *International Classification of Diseases* (ICD-10) define this set of disorders from mild to moderate to severe. The Institute for Health Metrics and Evaluation (IHME) adopt such definitions by disaggregating to mild, persistent depression (dysthymia) and major depressive disorder (severe).

25   WHO (1992). The ICD-10 classification of mental and behavioural disorders, Clinical descriptions and diagnostic guidelines 1992, cited in Ritchie, H. and Roser, M. (2020). Mental health. *Published online at OurWorldInData.org.* Retrieved on 16 April 2020 from https://ourworldindata.org/mental-health [online resource].

26   Munro, M. and Milne, R. (2020). Symptoms and causes of depression, and its diagnosis and management. *Nursing Times* [online], vol. 116, no. 4, pp. 18-22. Retrieved on 9 April 2020 from https://www.nursingtimes.net/roles/mental-health-nurses/symptoms-and-causes-of-depression-and-its-diagnosis-and-management-30-03-2020/.

27   Norman, I. and Ryrie. I. (2018). *The art and science of mental health nursing: Principles and practice*. London: Open University Press.

28   Dr. Grohol, J.M. (2018). *The five symptoms of depression*, 8 July 2018. Retrieved on 11 May 2020 from https://psychcentral.com/blog/the-five-symptoms-of-depression/.

29   Munro, M. and Milne, R. (2020). Symptoms and causes of depression, and its diagnosis and management. *Nursing Times* [online], vol. 116, no. 4, pp. 18-22. Retrieved on 9 April 2020 from https://www.

nursingtimes.net/roles/mental-health-nurses/symptoms-and-causes-of-depression-and-its-diagnosis-and-management-30-03-2020/.

30 Dr Grohol, J. M. (2016). *Depression*, 27 January 2020. Retrieved on 23 April 2020 from https://psychcentral.com/depression/.

31 Norman, I. and Ryrie, I. (2018). *The art and science of mental health nursing: Principles and practice.* London: Open University Press. See also, Munro, M. and Milne, R. (2020). Symptoms and causes of depression, and its diagnosis and management. *Nursing Times* [online], vol. 116, no. 4, pp. 18-22. Retrieved on 9 April 2020 from https://www.nursingtimes.net/roles/mental-health-nurses/symptoms-and-causes-of-depression-and-its-diagnosis-and-management-30-03-2020/.

32 World Health Organization (2020). *Depression fact sheet.* Retrieved on 9 April 2020 from https://www.who.int/news-room/fact-sheets/detail/depression; Australian Health Ministers (2009). *Fourth National Mental Health Plan – an agenda for collaborative government action in mental health 2009-2014.* Retrieved on 16 April 2020 from http://www.health.gov.au/internet/publications/publishing.nsf/Content/mental-pubs-f-plan09-toc; Munro, M. and Milne, R. (2020). Symptoms and causes of depression, and its diagnosis and management. *Nursing Times* [online], vol. 116, no. 4, pp. 18-22. Retrieved on 9 April 2020 from https://www.nursingtimes.net/roles/mental-health-nurses/symptoms-and-causes-of-depression-and-its-diagnosis-and-management-30-03-2020/.

33 Elwood, J. et al. (2019). A systematic review investigating if genetic or epigenetic markers are associated with postnatal depression. *Journal of Affective Disorders*, vol. 253, pp. 51-62. However, it must be noted that there is no one gene linked to depression: Munro, M. and Milne, R. (2020). Symptoms and causes of depression, and its diagnosis and management. *Nursing Times* [online], vol. 116, no. 4, pp. 18-22. Retrieved on 9 April 2020 from https://www.nursingtimes.net/roles/mental-health-nurses/symptoms-and-causes-of-depression-and-its-diagnosis-and-management-30-03-2020/.

34 Research has demonstrated that age, gender, education level, employment status and stage of the life-cycle are individual factors which may influence the prevalence of depression and, in terms of gender, the incidence of suicide from country to country, region to region: Ritchie, H. and Roser, M. (2020). Mental health. *Published online at OurWorldInData.org.* Retrieved on 16 April 2020 from https://ourworldindata.org/mental-health [online resource].

35 In all countries, the median estimate for the prevalence of depression is higher for women than for men. For example, Australia (M: 3.64%, F: 5.57%); Canada (M: 2.98%, F: 4.95%); New Zealand (M: 3.21%, F: 4.68%); United Kingdom (M: 3.29%, F: 4.12%); United States (M: 3.53%, F: 6.09%); World (M: 2.73%, F: 4.12%). Source: Ritchie, H. and Roser, M. (2020). Mental health. *Published online at OurWorldInData.org.* Retrieved on 16 April 2020 from https://ourworldindata.org/mental-health [online resource]; Global Burden of Disease Collaborative Network. Global Burden of Disease Study 2017 (GBD 2017). *Results.* Seattle, United States: Institute for Health Metrics and Evaluation (IHME).

36 Munro, M. and Milne, R. (2020). Symptoms and causes of depression, and its diagnosis and management. *Nursing Times* [online], vol. 116, no. 4, pp. 18-22. Retrieved on 9 April 2020 from https://www.nursingtimes.net/roles/mental-health-nurses/symptoms-and-causes-of-depression-and-its-diagnosis-and-management-30-03-2020/.

37 WHO (2012). *Risks to mental health: An overview of vulnerabilities and risk factors*; Ritchie, H. and Roser, M. (2020). Mental health. *Published online at OurWorldInData.org.* Retrieved on 16 April 2020 from https://ourworldindata.org/mental-health [online resource].

38 World Health Organization (2020). *Depression fact sheet*, 30 January 2020. Retrieved on 9 April 2020 from https://www.who.int/news-room/fact-sheets/detail/depression.

39 Munro, M. and Milne, R. (2020). Symptoms and causes of depression, and its diagnosis and management. *Nursing Times* [online], vol. 116, no. 4, pp. 18-22. Retrieved on 9 April 2020 from https://www.nursingtimes.net/roles/mental-health-nurses/symptoms-and-causes-of-depression-and-its-diagnosis-and-management-30-03-2020/; World Health Organization (2020). *Depression fact sheet*, 30 January 2020. Retrieved on 9 April 2020 from https://www.who.int/news-room/fact-sheets/detail/depression; Ritchie, H. and Roser, M. (2020). Mental health. *Published online at OurWorldInData.org.* Retrieved on 16 April 2020 from https://ourworldindata.org/mental-health [online resource].

40 Ritchie, H. and Roser, M. (2020). Mental health. *Published online at OurWorldInData.org.* Retrieved on 16 April 2020 from https://ourworldindata.org/mental-health [online resource].

41 Ibid.

42 Kessler, R.C. and Bromet, E.J. (2013). The epidemiology of depression across cultures. *Annual Review of Public Health*, no. 34, pp. 119-138.

43 Ritchie, H. and Roser, M. (2020). Mental health. *Published online at OurworldInData.org.* Retrieved on 16 April 2020 from https://ourworldindata.org/mental-health [online resource].

44 Ibid.

45 Ibid.

46 Hoebel, J. et al. (2017). Social inequalities and depressive symptoms in adults: The role of objective and subjective socioeconomic status. *PLoS ONE*, vol. 12, no. 1, e0169764.

47 Mind (2017). *Seeking help for a mental health problem.* Retrieved on 15 April 2020 from https://www.mind.org.uk/information-support/guides-to-support-and-services/seeking-help-for-a-mental-health-problem/helping-someone-else-seek-help/.

48 Munro, M. and Milne, R. (2020). Symptoms and causes of depression, and its diagnosis and management. *Nursing Times* [online], vol. 116, no. 4, pp. 18-22. Retrieved on 9 April 2020 from https://www.nursingtimes.net/roles/mental-health-nurses/symptoms-and-causes-of-depression-and-its-diagnosis-and-management-30-03-2020/.

49 Uher, R. and Pavlova, B. (2016). Long-term effects of depression treatment. *The Lancet Psychiatry*, vol. 3, no. 2, pp. 95-96.

50 Mulder, R. (2015). Depression relapse: Importance of a long-term perspective. *The Lancet*, vol. 386, no. 9988, pp. 10-12, cited in Munro, M. and Milne, R. (2020). Symptoms and causes of depression, and its diagnosis and management. *Nursing Times* [online], vol. 116, no. 4, pp. 18-22. Retrieved on 9 April 2020 from https://www.nursingtimes.net/roles/mental-health-nurses/symptoms-and-causes-of-depression-and-its-diagnosis-and-management-30-03-2020/.

51 American Psychiatric Association. (2000). *Diagnostic and Statistical Manual of Mental Disorders*. Text Revision - Fourth. Washington, D.C.: American Psychiatric Association.

52 Munro, M. and Milne, R. (2020). Symptoms and causes of depression, and its diagnosis and management. *Nursing Times* [online], vol. 116, no. 4, pp. 18-22. Retrieved on 9 April 2020 from https://www.nursingtimes.net/roles/mental-health-nurses/symptoms-and-causes-of-depression-and-its-diagnosis-and-management-30-03-2020/.

53 World Health Organization (2020). *Depression fact sheet*, 30 January 2020. Retrieved on 9 April 2020 from https://www.who.int/news-

room/fact-sheets/detail/depression; de Zwart, P.L. et al. (2018). Empirical evidence for definitions of episode, remission, recovery, relapse and recurrence in depression: A systematic review. *Epidemiology and Psychiatric Sciences*, vol. 28, no. 5, pp. 544-562.

54 Australian Bureau of Statistics (2018). *Causes of death*, 26 September 2018. Retrieved on 9 April 2020 from http://www.abs.gov.au/Causes-of-Death.

55 World Health Organization (2020). *Depression fact sheet*, 30 January 2020. Retrieved on 9 April 2020 from https://www.who.int/news-room/fact-sheets/detail/depression.

56 Gotlib, I. and Hammen, C. (2002). *Handbook of depression*. New York: Guilford Press; CDC (2020). *Preventing suicide*, Centers for Disease Control and Prevention. Updated 21 April 2020. Retrieved on 11 May 2020 from https://www.cdc.gov/violenceprevention/suicide/fastfact.html; CDC (2020). *10 leading causes of death and injury*, Centers for Disease Control and Prevention. Updated 30 March 2020. Retrieved on 11 May 2020 from https://www.cdc.gov/injury/wisqars/LeadingCauses.html.

57 Ferrari A.J. et al. (2014) The burden attributable to mental and substance use disorders as risk factors for suicide: Findings from the Global Burden of Disease Study 2010. *PLoS ONE*, vol. 9, no., e91936. https://doi.org/10.1371/journal.pone.0091936.

58 Brådvik, L. (2018). Suicide risk and mental disorders. *Int J Environ Res Public Health*, vol. 15, no. 9, p. 2028. doi: 10.3390/ijerph15092028; Inskip, H., Harris, E.C. and Barraclough, B. (1998). Lifetime risk of suicide for affective disorder, alcoholism and schizophrenia. *British Journal of Psychiatry*, no. 172, pp. 35–37. doi: 10.1192/bjp.172.1.35; Nordentoft, M., Mortensen, P.B. and Pedersen, C.B. (2011). Absolute risk of suicide after first hospital contact in mental disorder. *Arch. Gen. Psychiatry,* no. 68, pp. 1058–1064. doi: 10.1001/archgenpsychiatry.2011.113; CDC (2020). *Preventing suicide*, Centers for Disease Control and Prevention. Updated 21 April 2020. Retrieved on 11 May 2020 from https://www.cdc.gov/violenceprevention/suicide/fastfact.html; CDC (2020). *10 leading causes of death and injury*, Centers for Disease Control and Prevention. Updated 30 March 2020. Retrieved on 11 May 2020 from https://www.cdc.gov/injury/wisqars/LeadingCauses.html.

59 Munro, M. and Milne, R. (2020) Symptoms and causes of depression, and its diagnosis and management. *Nursing Times* [online], vol. 116, no. 4, pp. 18-22. Retrieved on 9 April 2020 from https://www.

nursingtimes.net/roles/mental-health-nurses/symptoms-and-causes-of-depression-and-its-diagnosis-and-management-30-03-2020/.

CHAPTER TWO

60   World Health Organization (2012). *Risks to mental health: An overview of vulnerabilities and risk factors,* 27 August 2012.

61   National Institute of Mental Health, *Depression*. Retrieved on 25 April 2020 from https://www.nimh.nih.gov/health/topics/depression/index.shtml.

62   Norman, I. and Ryrie, I. (2018). *The art and science of mental health nursing: Principles and practice*. London: Open University Press. Pietrangelo, A. (2018). *9 types of depression and how to recognize them.* Retrieved on 17 April 2020 from https://www.healthline.com/health/types-of-depression#depressive-psychosis.

63   Pietrangelo, A. (2018). *9 Types of depression and how to recognize them*. Retrieved on 17 April 2020 from https://www.healthline.com/health/types-of-depression#depressive-psychosis.

64   National Institute of Mental Health, *Depression*. Retrieved on 25 April 2020 from https://www.nimh.nih.gov/health/topics/depression/index.shtml.

65   For more information about the Black Dog Institute, visit their website at https://www.blackdoginstitute.org.au.

66   Black Dog Institute. Retrieved on 6 April 2020 from https://www.blackdoginstitute.org.au/about-us/who-we-are/our-logo.

67   Breckenridge, C. (2012). Leading Churchill myths – The myth of the "Black Dog", *Finest Hour 155*, Summer 2012. Retrieved on 28 April 2020 from https://winstonchurchill.org/publications/finest-hour/finest-hour-155/the-myth-of-the-black-dog/.

68   Ibid.

69   National Institute of Mental Health, *Depression*. Retrieved on 25 April 2020 from https://www.nimh.nih.gov/health/topics/depression/index.shtml.

70   Li, W., Mai, X. and Liu, C. (2014). The default mode network and social understanding of others: What do brain connectivity studies tell us. *Front Hum Neurosci*. no. 8, p. 74.

71   American Psychological Association. (2020). *Anxiety*. Retrieved on 29 April 2020 from https://www.apa.org/topics/anxiety/.

72   Hranov, L.G. (2007). Comorbid anxiety and depression: Illumination of a controversy. *International Journal of Psychiatry in Clinical Practice*, vol.

11, no. 3, pp. 171-189. World Health Organization (2020). *Depression.* Retrieved on 29 April 2020 from https://www.who.int/news-room/fact-sheets/detail/depression.

73 Cameron, O.G. (2007). Understanding comorbid depression and anxiety. *Psychiatric Times*, no. 24, p. 14.

74 Hofmeijer-Sevink, M.K. et al. (2012). Clinical relevance of comorbidity in anxiety disorders: A report from the Netherlands Study of Depression and Anxiety (NESDA). *Journal of Affective Disorders*, vol. 137, no. 1-3, pp. 106-112.

75 World Health Organization (2020). *Depression.* Retrieved on 29 April 2020 from https://www.who.int/news-room/fact-sheets/detail/depression.

76 Australian Bureau of Statistics (2008). *National Survey of Mental Health and Wellbeing: Summary of results,* 2007, p. 27.

77 *Depression and Other Common Mental Disorders: Global Health Estimates.* (2017). Geneva: World Health Organization. Licence: CC BY-NC-SA3.0 IGO.

CHAPTER THREE

78 World Health Organization (2020). *Depression fact sheet*, 30 January 2020. Retrieved on 9 April 2020 from https://www.who.int/news-room/fact-sheets/detail/depression.

79 WHO (2005). *Mental health policies and programmes in the workplace.* WHO Press, Geneva.

80 Sastre, R.M. et al. (2019). Instruments to assess mental health-related stigma among health professionals and students in health sciences: A systematic psychometric review. *Journal of Advanced Nursing*, vol. 75, no. 9, pp. 1838-1853.

81 National Institute for Health and Care Excellence (2009). *Depression in adults: Recognition and management.* NICE. National Institute for Health and Care Excellence (2009). *Depression in adults with a chronic physical health problem: Recognition and management. NICE.*

82 Beyond Blue Ltd, *Information Paper – Stigma and discrimination associated with depression and anxiety*, August 2015.

83 Ibid.

84 TNS Social Research (2014). *State of workplace mental health in Australia.* Beyondblue and TNS Social Research.

85 TNS Social Research (2014). *State of workplace mental health in Australia.* Beyondblue and TNS Social Research, p.7.

86 Ruby Wax is an author and comedian. In 2015, she was awarded an OBE for her services to mental health.

87 Morgan, E. (2015). Should you tell your boss about mental health illness? Absolutely. *The Guardian*, 7 July 2015.

88 Ibid.

89 Dr Grohol, J.M. (2018). *The five symptoms of depression*, 8 July 2018. Retrieved on 12 May 2020 from https://psychcentral.com/blog/the-five-symptoms-of-depression/.

90 Sastre, R.M. et al. (2019). Instruments to assess mental health-related stigma among health professionals and students in health sciences: A systematic psychometric review. *Journal of Advanced Nursing*, vol. 75, no. 9, pp.1838-1853.

91 The Royal Australian College of General Practitioners (2019). *Accounting for 65% of common ailments dealt with by doctors in general practice*. General Practice: Health of the Nation 2019. East Melbourne.

92 Britt, H. et al. (2016). General practice activity in Australia 2015–16. General practice series no. 40. Sydney: Sydney University Press, 2016. Retrieved on 12 May 2020 from https://ses.library.usyd.edu.au/bitstream/2123/15514/5/9781743325148_ONLINE.pdf.

93 The treatment rate increased significantly to 46% in 2009-10: Whiteford, H.A. et al. (2014). Estimating treatment rates for mental disorders in Australia. *Australian Health Review*, no. 38, pp. 80-85.

94 Australian Bureau of Statistics (2008). *National Survey of Mental Health and Wellbeing: Summary of Results, 2007*, p.44.

CHAPTER FOUR

95 Munro, M. and Milne, R. (2020). Symptoms and causes of depression, and its diagnosis and management. *Nursing Times* [online], vol. 116, no. 4, pp. 18-22. Retrieved on 9 April 2020 from https://www.nursingtimes.net/roles/mental-health-nurses/symptoms-and-causes-of-depression-and-its-diagnosis-and-management-30-03-2020/.

96 Ibid.

97 Cruwys, T. et al. (2013). Social group memberships protect against future depression, alleviate depression symptoms, and prevent depression relapse. *Social Science and Medicine*, no. 98, pp. 179-186; Rosenbaum S et al. (2014). Physical activity interventions for people with mental illness: a systematic review and meta-analysis. *Journal of Science and Medicine in Sport*, vol. 18, no. 9, p. e150; Pfeiffer, P.N.

et al. (2011). Efficacy of peer support interventions for depression: A meta-analysis. *General Hospital Psychiatry*, vol. 33, no. 1, pp. 29-36.

98 Gelenberg, A.J. et al. (2010). *Practice guideline for the treatment of patients with major depressive disorder.* American Psychiatric Association; Ekers, D. and Webster, L. (2012). An overview of the effectiveness of psychological therapy for depression and stepped care service delivery models. *Journal of Research in Nursing*, vol. 18, no. 2, pp. 171-184; and Kellner, C.H. et al. (2012). ECT in treatment-resistant depression. *American Journal of Psychiatry*, vol. 169, no. 12, pp. 1238-1244.

99 Sanchez-Villegas, A. and Martínez-González, M.A. (2013). Diet, a new target to prevent depression? *BMC Medicine*, vol. 11, no. 3.

100 Rosenbaum, S. et al. (2014). Physical activity interventions for people with mental illness: A systematic review and meta-analysis. *Journal of Science and Medicine in Sport*, vol. 18, no. 9, p. e150.

101 Ekers, D. and Webster, L. (2012). An overview of the effectiveness of psychological therapy for depression and stepped care service delivery models. Journal of Research in Nursing, vol. 18, no. 2, pp. 171-184.

102 Dr Grohol, J.M. (2020). *Depression,* 28 April 2020. Retrieved on 12 May 2020 from https://psychcentral.com/depression/#treatment.

103 Munro, M. and Milne, R. (2020). Symptoms and causes of depression, and its diagnosis and management. *Nursing Times* [online], vol. 116, no. 4, pp. 18-22. Retrieved on 9 April 2020 from https://www.nursingtimes.net/roles/mental-health-nurses/symptoms-and-causes-of-depression-and-its-diagnosis-and-management-30-03-2020/.

104 National Institute of Mental Health, *Depression*. Retrieved on 25 April 2020 from https://www.nimh.nih.gov/health/topics/depression/index.shtml.

105 Ibid.

106 Dr Grohol, J.M (2020). *Depression*, 28 April 2020. Retrieved on 12 May 2020 from https://psychcentral.com/depression/.

107 Zhang, A. et al. (2019). The effectiveness of four empirically supported psychotherapies for primary care depression and anxiety: A systematic review and meta-analysis. *Journal of Affective Disorders*, no. 245, pp. 1168-1186.

108 Gelenberg, A.J. et al. (2010). Practice guideline for the treatment of patients with major depressive disorder. *American Psychiatric Association*; World Health Organization, *Depression fact sheet*, 30

January 2020. Retrieved on 9 April 2020 from https://www.who.int/news-room/fact-sheets/detail/depression.

109 Dr Grohol, J.M (2020). *Depression*, 28 April 2020. Retrieved on 12 May 2020 from https://psychcentral.com/depression/.

110 Sarris, J. (2007). Herbal medicines in the treatment of psychiatric disorders: A systematic review. *Phytother. Res.*, no. 21, pp. 703-716. doi:10.1002/ptr.2187.

111 National Institute of Mental Health, *Depression*. Retrieved on 25 April 2020 from https://www.nimh.nih.gov/health/topics/depression/index.shtml.

112 Ibid.

113 Kellner C.H. et al. (2012). ECT in treatment-resistant depression. *American Journal of Psychiatry*, vol. 169, no. 12, pp. 1238-1244; National Institute of Mental Health, *Depression*. Retrieved on 25 April 2020 from https://www.nimh.nih.gov/health/topics/depression/index.shtml.

114 The process of providing education and information to people seeking or receiving mental health services and their families: Munro, M. and Milne, R. (2020). Symptoms and causes of depression, and its diagnosis and management. *Nursing Times* [online], vol. 116, no. 4, pp. 18-22. Retrieved on 9 April 2020 from https://www.nursingtimes.net/roles/mental-health-nurses/symptoms-and-causes-of-depression-and-its-diagnosis-and-management-30-03-2020/.

115 National Institute for Health and Care Excellence (2009). *Depression in adults: recognition and management*. NICE; National Institute for Health and Care Excellence (2009). *Depression in adults with a chronic physical health problem: Recognition and management*. NICE.

116 Dr Grohol, J.M. (2020). *Depression*, 28 April 2020. Retrieved on 12 May 2020 from https://psychcentral.com/depression/; National Institute of Mental Health, *Depression*. Retrieved on 25 April 2020 from https://www.nimh.nih.gov/health/topics/depression/index.shtml.

117 Munro, M. and Milne, R. (2020). Symptoms and causes of depression, and its diagnosis and management. *Nursing Times* [online], vol. 116, no. 4, pp. 18-22. Retrieved on 9 April 2020 from https://www.nursingtimes.net/roles/mental-health-nurses/symptoms-and-causes-of-depression-and-its-diagnosis-and-management-30-03-2020/.

118 Rosenbaum, S. et al. (2014). Physical activity interventions for people with mental illness: A systematic review and meta-analysis. *Journal of Science and Medicine in Sport*, vol. 18, no. 9, p. e150; Sanchez-Villegas,

A. and Martínez-González, M.A. (2013). Diet, a new target to prevent depression? *BMC Medicine*, no. 11, p. 3.

119 Mental Health Foundation (2016). *Mental health in Scotland: Fundamental facts 2016.* MHF. Retrieved on 12 May 2020 from https://www.mentalhealth.org.uk/publications/mental-health-scotland-fundamental-facts.

120 Rosenbaum, S. et al. (2014). Physical activity interventions for people with mental illness: A systematic review and meta-analysis. *Journal of Science and Medicine in Sport*, vol. 18, no. 9, p. e150; Sanchez-Villegas, A. and Martínez-González, M.A. (2013). Diet, a new target to prevent depression? *BMC Medicine*, no. 11, p. 3; Cruwys, T. et al. (2013). Social group memberships protect against future depression, alleviate depression symptoms and prevent depression relapse. *Social Science and Medicine*, no. 98, pp. 179-186; Pfeiffer, P.N. et al. (2011). Efficacy of peer support interventions for depression: A meta-analysis. *General Hospital Psychiatry*, vol. 33, no. 1, pp. 29-36.

121 National Institute of Mental Health, *Depression*. Retrieved on 25 April 2020 from https://www.nimh.nih.gov/health/topics/depression/index.shtml.

122 Ibid.

123 Munro, M. and Milne, R. (2020). Symptoms and causes of depression, and its diagnosis and management. *Nursing Times* [online], vol. 116, no. 4, pp. 18-22. Retrieved on 9 April 2020 from https://www.nursingtimes.net/roles/mental-health-nurses/symptoms-and-causes-of-depression-and-its-diagnosis-and-management-30-03-2020/; Loos, S. et al. (2017). Recovery and decision-making involvement in people with severe mental illness from six countries: A prospective observational study. *BMC Psychiatry*, vol. 17, no. 1, p. 38.

124 Dr Grohol, J.M. (2020). *Depression*, 28 April 2020. Retrieved on 12 May 2020 from https://psychcentral.com/depression/.

125 Uher, R. and Pavlova, B. (2016). Long-term effects of depression treatment. *The Lancet Psychiatry*, vol. 3, no. 2, pp. 95-96.

126 Scottish Recovery Network, NHS Education for Scotland. (2007). *Realising Recovery: A National Framework for Learning and Training in Recovery-Focused Practice.* SRN.

CHAPTER FIVE

127 Burcusa, S.L. and Iacono, W.G. (2007). Risk for recurrence in depression, *Clinical Psychology Review*, vol. 27, no. 8, pp. 959-985, published online 2007 Mar 3. doi 10.1016/j.cpr.2007.02.005.

128 In adults, these risk factors derive from several clinical and family history variables. To date, several variables have been identified as risk factors for recurrence in adults deriving from the clinical picture (age at onset/number of episodes, severity, comorbidity), family history, cognitions, personality (neuroticism), poor social support, and stressful life events. See, for example, Jumnoodoo, R. et al. (2017). Using sustained recovery and relapse in mental health. *Nursing Times*, vol. 113, no. 12, pp. 56-58. See also Burcusa, S.L and Iacono, W.G. (2007). Risk for recurrence in depression. Clinical Psychology Review, vol. 27, no. 8, pp. 959-985, published online 2007 Mar 3. doi 10.1016/j.cpr.2007.02.005.

129 Examples of apps include *BeyondNow* by Australian Monash University and Beyond Blue Ltd), *iBobbly* by the Black Dog Institute in Australia, *Stay Alive* by Grassroots Suicide Prevention (UK) and the *Suicide Prevention App* by ISD Innovations, Inc. (US).

130 For a discussion on the benefits of practising yoga, for example, see Shapiro, D. et al. (2007). Yoga as a complimentary treatment of depression: Effects of traits and moods on treatment outcome. *Evidence Based Complementary Alternate Medicine,* vol. 4, no. 4, pp 493-502.

CHAPTER SIX

131 Theoretical orientation describes what theories the clinician subscribes to in thinking about a person's problems and how best to treat them: Dr Grohol, J.M. (2015). *How to choose a therapist and other questions about Psychotherapy*, updated 15 May 2019. Retrieved on 5 May 2020 from https://psychcentral.com/lib/how-to-choose-a-therapist-and-other-questions-about-psychotherapy/. Examples of approaches to treatment based on theoretical orientation are Psychodynamic (and psychoanalytic); Cognitive-behavioural; Humanistic (and existential); and Eclectic: Dr Grohol, J.M. (2019). *Types of Psychotherapy: Theoretical orientations & practices of therapists*, 15 May 2019. Retrieved on 12 May 2020 from https://psychcentral.com/lib/types-of-therapies-theoretical-orientations-and-practices-of-therapists/.

132 Wong, K. (2017). *How to find a therapist*. Retrieved on 5 May 2020 from https://www.thecut.com/2017/12/a-beginners-guide-to-finding-the-right-therapist.html.

133 Good Therapy Australia, *Types of therapists*. Retrieved on 5 May 2020 from https://www.goodtherapy.com.au/flex/types-of-therapists/906/1.

134 For a discussion of these differences see, for example, Good Therapy Australia, *Types of therapists* at https://www.goodtherapy.com.au/flex/types-of-therapists/906/1.

135 Grohol, J.M. (2015). *How to choose a therapist and other questions about Psychotherapy*, updated 15 May 2019. Retrieved on 5 May 2020 from https://psychcentral.com/lib/how-to-choose-a-therapist-and-other-questions-about-psychotherapy/.

136 For example, the American Psychological Association, Psychotherapy and Counselling Federation of Australia, Australian Psychological Society and Royal Australian and New Zealand College of Psychiatrists.

137 In Australia, depression and anxiety have been reported to be more common than coughs and colds, with research finding that one in eight visits to GPs are related to mental health issues: *General Practice Health of the Nation Report 2019* accounting for 65% of common ailments dealt with by doctors in general practice; and University of Sydney, General Practice Activity in Australia 2015-2016.

138 For example, the American Psychological Association, Psychotherapy and Counselling Federation of Australia, Australian Psychological Society and Royal Australian and New Zealand College of Psychiatrists.

139 Hamde, M. (2018). *ABC Life. Finding the right psychologist for your mental health needs*, posted 10 September 2018, updated 25 February 2020. Retrieved on 5 May 2020 from https://www.abc.net.au/life/finding-the-right-psychologist/10139160.

140 Ibid.

141 Hamde, M. (2018). *ABC Life. Finding the right psychologist for your mental health needs*, posted 10 September 2018, updated 25 February 2020. Retrieved on 5 May 2020 from https://www.abc.net.au/life/finding-the-right-psychologist/10139160; Shedler, J. Ph.D. (2016). How to choose a therapist, *Psychology Today* posted 16 April 2016. Retrieved on 5 May 2020 from https://www.psychologytoday.com/au/blog/psychologically-minded/201604/how-choose-therapist.

142 Grohol, J.M. (2015). *How to choose a therapist and other questions about Psychotherapy*, updated 15 May 2019. Retrieved on 5 May 2020 from https://psychcentral.com/lib/how-to-choose-a-therapist-and-other-questions-about-psychotherapy/.

143 Good Therapy Australia, *Choosing a therapist*. Retrieved on 5 May 2020 from https://www.goodtherapy.com.au/flex/choosing-a-therapist/101/1.

144 Borchard, T.J. (2019). *12 ways to keep going with depression*. Retrieved on 6 May 2020 from https://psychcentral.com/blog/12-ways-to-keep-going-with-depression/.

145 Grohol, J.M. (2015). *How to choose a therapist and other questions about Psychotherapy*, updated 15 May 2019. Retrieved on 5 May 2020 from https://psychcentral.com/lib/how-to-choose-a-therapist-and-other-questions-about-psychotherapy/.

146 American Psychological Association (2020). *How to choose a Psychologist*. Retrieved on 5 May 2020 from https://www.apa.org/helpcenter/choose-therapist.

147 Grohol, J.M. (2015). *How to choose a therapist and other questions about Psychotherapy*, updated 15 May 2019. Retrieved on 5 May 2020 from https://psychcentral.com/lib/how-to-choose-a-therapist-and-other-questions-about-psychotherapy/.

148 Hamde, M. (2018). *ABC Life. Finding the right psychologist for your mental health needs*, posted 10 September 2018, updated 25 February 2020. Retrieved on 5 May 2020 from https://www.abc.net.au/life/finding-the-right-psychologist/10139160.

149 Wong, K. (2017). *How to find a therapist*. Retrieved on 5 May 2020 from https://www.thecut.com/2017/12/a-beginners-guide-to-finding-the-right-therapist.html.

150 Grohol, J.M. (2015). *How to choose a therapist and other questions about Psychotherapy,* updated 15 May 2019. Retrieved on 5 May 2020 from https://psychcentral.com/lib/how-to-choose-a-therapist-and-other-questions-about-psychotherapy/.

151 Ibid.

152 Ibid.

153 American Psychological Association (2020). *How to choose a psychologist*, retrieved on 5 May 2020 from https://www.apa.org/helpcenter/choose-therapist.

154 Sliding scale fees are variable prices for products, services, or taxes based on a customer's ability to pay.

155 Medicare is the scheme that gives Australian residents access to healthcare. It gives all Australians and some people from overseas a wide

range of health and hospital services at no cost or low cost: https://www.healthdirect.gov.au/what-is-medicare. If your country has a national health scheme, you could substitute the name of it for Medicare. If not, you could simply use the appropriate reference. The objective of this question is to find out what payment methods are accepted by the practice so that you can have certainty that you can afford the treatment and it is the 'right' option for you.

156 Medicaid provides health coverage to millions of Americans, including eligible low-income adults, children, pregnant women, elderly adults, and people with disabilities. Medicaid is administered by states, according to federal requirements. The program is funded jointly by states and the federal government: https://www.medicaid.gov/medicaid/index.html. If your country has a national health scheme, you could substitute the name of it for Medicaid. If not, you could simply use the appropriate reference. As observed in the preceding note, the objective of this question is to find out what payment methods are accepted by the practice so that you can have certainty that you can afford the treatment and it is the 'right' option for you.

157 Grohol, J.M. (2015). How to choose a therapist and other questions about psychotherapy, updated 15 May 2019. Retrieved on 5 May 2020 from https://psychcentral.com/lib/how-to-choose-a-therapist-and-other-questions-about-psychotherapy/.

158 Good Therapy Australia, *Choosing a therapist*. Retrieved on 5 May 2020 from https://www.goodtherapy.com.au/flex/choosing-a-therapist/101/1.

159 Ibid.

160 For more information, see Good Therapy Australia, *Choosing a therapist* at https://www.goodtherapy.com.au/flex/choosing-a-therapist/101/1.

161 Shedler. J. Ph.D. (2016). How to choose a therapist, *Psychology Today*, posted 16 April 2016. Retrieved on 5 May 2020 from https://www.psychologytoday.com/au/blog/psychologically-minded/201604/how-choose-therapist.

162 Alpert, J. (2012). *Be fearless: Change your life in 28 days*, Hodder & Stoughton, 26 April 2012.

163 Ibid.

164 Wong, K. (2017). *How to find a therapist*. Retrieved on 5 May 2020 from https://www.thecut.com/2017/12/a-beginners-guide-to-finding-the-right-therapist.html.

165 Ibid.

166 In most countries, this conduct would be reportable to the relevant regulatory authorities.
167 This is fundamental to the relationship and may warrant report to the relevant professional or licensing body in your location.
168 Horvath, A. O. and Luborsky, L. (1993). The role of the therapeutic alliance in psychotherapy. *Journal of Consulting and Clinical Psychology*, vol. 61, no. 4, pp. 561-573.
169 Shedler, J. Ph.D. (2016). How to choose a therapist, *Psychology Today*, posted 16 April 2016. Retrieved on 5 May 2020 from https://www.psychologytoday.com/au/blog/psychologically-minded/201604/how-choose-therapist.
170 Ibid.
171 Ibid.
172 Ibid.
173 See for example, Grohol, J.M. (2015). *How to choose a therapist and other questions about psychotherapy*, updated 15 May 2019. Retrieved on 5 May 2020 from https://psychcentral.com/lib/how-to-choose-a-therapist-and-other-questions-about-psychotherapy/; Shedler, J. Ph.D. (2016). How to choose a therapist, *Psychology Today*, posted 16 April 2016. Retrieved on 5 May 2020 from https://www.psychologytoday.com/au/blog/psychologically-minded/201604/how-choose-therapist; Wong, K. (2017). *A beginner's guide to finding the right therapist*, 1 December 2017. Retrieved on 5 May 2020 from https://www.thecut.com/2017/12/a-beginners-guide-to-finding-the-right-therapist.html; Hamde, M. ABC Life. *Finding the right psychologist for your mental health needs*, posted 10 September 2018, updated 25 February 2020. Retrieved on 5 May 2020 from https://www.abc.net.au/life/finding-the-right-psychologist/10139160.
174 Shedler, J. Ph.D. (2016). How to choose a therapist, *Psychology Today*, posted 16 April 2016. Retrieved on 5 May 2020 from https://www.psychologytoday.com/au/blog/psychologically-minded/201604/how-choose-therapist.
175 Ibid.
176 Wong, K. (2017). *A beginner's guide to finding the right therapist*, 1 December 2017. Retrieved on 5 May 2020 from https://www.thecut.com/2017/12/a-beginners-guide-to-finding-the-right-therapist.html.
177 Ibid.
178 Ibid.

179 Grohol, J.M. (2015). *How to choose a therapist and other questions about psychotherapy*, updated 15 May 2019. Retrieved on 5 May 2020 from https://psychcentral.com/lib/how-to-choose-a-therapist-and-other-questions-about-psychotherapy/.

180 American Psychological Association (2020). *How to choose a psychologist.* Retrieved on 5 May 2020 from https://www.apa.org/helpcenter/choose-therapist.

181 Ibid.

182 These questions appear in Hamde, M. (2018). *ABC Life. Finding the right psychologist for your mental health needs,* posted 10 September 2018, updated 25 February 2020. Retrieved on 5 May 2020 from https://www.abc.net.au/life/finding-the-right-psychologist/10139160.

183 These were adapted from the best-practice principles for health professionals espoused by the National Institute for Health and Care Excellence (2009). *Depression in adults: Recognition and management.* NICE; National Institute for Health and Care Excellence (2009). *Depression in adults with a chronic physical health problem: Recognition and management,* cited in Munro, M. and Milne, R. (2020). Symptoms and causes of depression, and its diagnosis and management. *Nursing Times* [online], vol. 116, no. 4, pp. 18-22. Retrieved on 9 April 2020 from https://www.nursingtimes.net/roles/mental-health-nurses/symptoms-and-causes-of-depression-and-its-diagnosis-and-management-30-03-2020/.

CHAPTER SEVEN

184 Schimelpfening, N. (2020). *The worst things to say to someone who is depressed.* Retrieved on 6 May 2020 from https://www.verywellmind.com/worst-things-to-say-to-someone-who-is-depressed-1066982.

185 For example, see Beyond Blue Ltd, What not to say to someone with depression. Retrieved on 6 May 2020 from https://www.beyondblue.org.au/personal-best/pillar/supporting-others/what-not-to-say-to-someone-with-depression; Psych Central, *Worst things to say to someone who's depressed,* 8 October 2018. Retrieved on 6 May 2020 from https://psychcentral.com/lib/worst-things-to-say-to-someone-whos-depressed/; Schimelpfening, N. (2020). *The worst things to say to someone who is depressed,* 25 March 2020. Retrieved on 6 May 2020 from https://www.verywellmind.com/worst-things-to-say-to-someone-who-is-depressed-1066982; Hurley, K. (2018). *Helping someone with depression: What people want to hear (and what they don't),* 13 February

2018. Retrieved on 6 May 2020 from https://www.psycom.net/5-phrases-to-help-someone-with-depression; Psych Central, *Best things to say to someone who's depressed*. 19 June 2019. Retrieved on 6 May 2020 from https://psychcentral.com/lib/best-things-to-say-to-someone-whos-depressed/; Schimelpfening, N. (2020). *What to say when someone is depressed*. Retrieved on 6 May 2020 from https://www.verywellmind.com/what-to-say-when-someone-is-depressed-1067474#citation-8; Thomas, F. (2020). *10 things to say to someone with depression*. Retrieved on 6 May 2020 from https://www.headstogether.org.uk/10-things-to-say-to-someone-with-depression/.

186 Schimelpfening, N. (2020). *The worst things to say to someone who is depressed*, 25 March 2020. Retrieved on 6 May 2020 from https://www.verywellmind.com/worst-things-to-say-to-someone-who-is-depressed-1066982.

187 Psych Central, *Worst things to say to someone who's depressed*, 8 October 2018. Retrieved on 6 May 2020 from https://psychcentral.com/lib/worst-things-to-say-to-someone-whos-depressed/.

188 Ibid.

189 Schimelpfening, N. (2020). *The worst things to say to someone who is depressed*. Retrieved on 6 May 2020 from https://www.verywellmind.com/worst-things-to-say-to-someone-who-is-depressed-1066982.

190 Beyond Blue Ltd. *What not to say to someone with depression*. Retrieved on 6 May 2020 from https://www.beyondblue.org.au/personal-best/pillar/supporting-others/what-not-to-say-to-someone-with-depression.

191 Schimelpfening, N. (2020). *The worst things to say to someone who is depressed*. Retrieved on 6 May 2020 from https://www.verywellmind.com/worst-things-to-say-to-someone-who-is-depressed-1066982.

192 Beyond Blue Ltd. *What not to say to someone with depression*. Retrieved on 6 May 2020 from https://www.beyondblue.org.au/personal-best/pillar/supporting-others/what-not-to-say-to-someone-with-depression.

193 Psych Central, *Best things to say to someone who's depressed*, 19 June 2019. Retrieved on 6 May 2020 from https://psychcentral.com/lib/best-things-to-say-to-someone-whos-depressed/.

194 Find Your Words (2020). *What to say to someone who's depressed*. Retrieved on 6 May 2020 from https://findyourwords.org/support-someone-with-depression/what-to-say-to-someone/.

195 Schimelpfening, N. (2020). *The worst things to say to someone who is depressed*, 25 March 2020. Retrieved on 6 May 2020 from https://www.verywellmind.com/worst-things-to-say-to-someone-who-is-depressed-1066982; Conner K.O, Copeland V.C, Grote N.K. et al. (2010). Mental health treatment seeking among older adults with depression: The impact of stigma and race. *American Journal of Geriatric Psychiatry*, vol. 18, no. 6, pp. 531-543. doi:10.1097/JGP.0b013e3181cc0366.

196 Young, K. *What to say (and not to say) to someone who's depressed*. Retrieved on 6 May 2020 from https://www.heysigmund.com/what-to-say-to-someone-who-is-depressed/.

197 Ibid.

198 Find Your Words (2020). *What to say to someone who's depressed*. Retrieved on 6 May 2020 from https://findyourwords.org/support-someone-with-depression/what-to-say-to-someone/.

199 Munro, M. and Milne, R. (2020). Symptoms and causes of depression, and its diagnosis and management. *Nursing Times* [online], vol. 116, no. 4, pp. 18-22. Retrieved on 9 April 2020 from https://www.nursingtimes.net/roles/mental-health-nurses/symptoms-and-causes-of-depression-and-its-diagnosis-and-management-30-03-2020/.

200 Brands, B., Sproule, B. and Marshman, J. (Eds.) (1998). *Drugs & drug abuse* (3rd Ed.) Ontario: Addiction Research Foundation.

201 Psych Central, *What not to say to a depressed person*. Retrieved on 8 May 2020 from https://psychcentral.com/blog/what-not-to-say-to-a-depressed-person/.

202 Young, K. *What to say (and not to say) to someone who's depressed*. Retrieved on 6 May 2020 from https://www.heysigmund.com/what-to-say-to-someone-who-is-depressed/.

203 Psych Central, *What not to say to a depressed person*. Retrieved on 8 May 2020 from https://psychcentral.com/blog/what-not-to-say-to-a-depressed-person/.

204 Ibid.

205 Young, K. *What to say (and not to say) to someone who's depressed*. Retrieved on 6 May 2020 from https://www.heysigmund.com/what-to-say-to-someone-who-is-depressed/.

206 Schimelpfening, N. (2020). *The worst things to say to someone who is depressed*, 25 March 2020. Retrieved on 6 May 2020 from https://

www.verywellmind.com/worst-things-to-say-to-someone-who-is-depressed-1066982.

207 Ibid.

208 Orzechowska, A. et al. (2013). Depression and ways of coping with stress: A preliminary study. *Medical Science Monitor*, vol. 2013, no. 19, pp. 1050–1056. doi:10.12659/MSM.889778.

209 Schimelpfening, N. (2020). *The worst things to say to someone who is depressed*, 25 March 2020. Retrieved on 6 May 2020 from https://www.verywellmind.com/worst-things-to-say-to-someone-who-is-depressed-1066982.

210 Hurley, K. (2018). *Helping someone with depression: What people want to hear (and what they don't)*. Retrieved on 6 May 2020 from https://www.psycom.net/5-phrases-to-help-someone-with-depression.

211 Beyond Blue Ltd. *What not to say to someone with depression*. Retrieved on 6 May 2020 from https://www.beyondblue.org.au/personal-best/pillar/supporting-others/what-not-to-say-to-someone-with-depression.

212 Beyond Blue Ltd, (2020). *What to say and why*. Retrieved on 6 May 2020 from https://www.beyondblue.org.au/get-support/have-the-conversation/what-to-say-and-why.

213 Hurley, K. (2018). *Helping someone with depression: What people want to hear (and what they don't)*. Retrieved on 6 May 2020 from https://www.psycom.net/5-phrases-to-help-someone-with-depression.

214 Young, K. *What to say (and not to say) to someone who's depressed*. Retrieved on 6 May 2020 from https://www.heysigmund.com/what-to-say-to-someone-who-is-depressed/.

215 Hurley, K. (2018). *Helping someone with depression: What people want to hear (and what they don't)*. Retrieved on 6 May 2020 from https://www.psycom.net/5-phrases-to-help-someone-with-depression.

216 Schimelpfening, N. (2020). *The worst things to say to someone who is depressed*. Retrieved on 6 May 2020 from https://www.verywellmind.com/worst-things-to-say-to-someone-who-is-depressed-1066982.

217 Conner K.O. et al. (2010). Mental health treatment seeking among older adults with depression: the impact of stigma and race. *American Journal Geriatric Psychiatry*, vol. 18, no. 6, pp. 531-543. doi:10.1097/JGP.0b013e3181cc0366 cited in Schimelpfening, N. (2020). *What to say when someone is depressed*. Retrieved on 6 May 2020 from https://www.verywellmind.com/what-to-say-when-someone-is-depressed-

1067474#citation-8. See also Psych Central, *Best things to say to someone who's depressed*. 19 June 2019. Retrieved on 6 May 2020 from https://psychcentral.com/lib/best-things-to-say-to-someone-whos-depressed/.

218 Trivedi, M.H. (2004). The link between depression and physical symptoms. *Prim Care Companion J Clin Psychiatry*, vol. 6(Suppl 1), pp. 12-16.

219 Hurley, K. (2018). *Helping someone with depression: What people want to hear (and what they don't)*. Retrieved on 6 May 2020 from https://www.psycom.net/5-phrases-to-help-someone-with-depression.

220 Schimelpfening, N. (2020). *The worst things to say to someone who is depressed*. Retrieved on 6 May 2020 from https://www.verywellmind.com/worst-things-to-say-to-someone-who-is-depressed-1066982.

221 Ibid.

222 Hurley, K. (2018). *Helping someone with depression: What people want to hear (and what they don't)*. Retrieved on 6 May 2020 from https://www.psycom.net/5-phrases-to-help-someone-with-depression.

223 Beyond Blue Ltd. *What not to say to someone with depression*. Retrieved on 6 May 2020 from https://www.beyondblue.org.au/personal-best/pillar/supporting-others/what-not-to-say-to-someone-with-depression.

224 Schimelpfening, N. (2020). *The worst things to say to someone who is depressed*. Retrieved on 6 May 2020 from https://www.verywellmind.com/worst-things-to-say-to-someone-who-is-depressed-1066982; Young, K. *What to say (and not to say) to someone who's depressed*. Retrieved on 6 May 2020 from https://www.heysigmund.com/what-to-say-to-someone-who-is-depressed/.

225 Schimelpfening, N. (2020). *The worst things to say to someone who is depressed*. Retrieved on 6 May 2020 from https://www.verywellmind.com/worst-things-to-say-to-someone-who-is-depressed-1066982.

226 Young, K. *What to say (and not to say) to someone who's depressed*. Retrieved on 6 May 2020 from https://www.heysigmund.com/what-to-say-to-someone-who-is-depressed.

227 Ibid.

228 Hurley, K. (2018). *Helping someone with depression: What people want to hear (and what they don't)*. Retrieved on 6 May 2020 from https://www.psycom.net/5-phrases-to-help-someone-with-depression.

229 Beyond Blue Ltd. *What not to say to someone with depression*. Retrieved on 6 May 2020 from https://www.beyondblue.org.au/personal-

best/pillar/supporting-others/what-not-to-say-to-someone-with-depression.

230 Hurley, K. (2018). Helping someone with depression: What people want to hear (and what they don't). Retrieved on 6 May 2020 from https://www.psycom.net/5-phrases-to-help-someone-with-depression.

231 Thomas, F. (2020). *10 things to say to someone with depression*. Retrieved on 6 May 2020 from https://www.headstogether.org.uk/10-things-to-say-to-someone-with-depression/.

232 Beyond Blue Ltd. *What not to say to someone with depression*. Retrieved on 6 May 2020 from https://www.beyondblue.org.au/personal-best/pillar/supporting-others/what-not-to-say-to-someone-with-depression.

233 Andrews, G. (2001). Should depression be managed as a chronic disease? *BMJ*, vol. 322, no. 7283, pp. 419-21. doi:10.1136/bmj.322.7283.419.

234 Schimelpfening, N. (2020). *The worst things to say to someone who is depressed*. Retrieved on 6 May 2020 from https://www.verywellmind.com/worst-things-to-say-to-someone-who-is-depressed-1066982.

235 Thomas, F. (2020). *10 things to say to someone with depression*. Retrieved on 6 May 2020 from https://www.headstogether.org.uk/10-things-to-say-to-someone-with-depression/.

236 Young K. *What to say (and not to say) to someone who's depressed*. Retrieved on 6 May 2020 from https://www.heysigmund.com/what-to-say-to-someone-who-is-depressed/.

237 Ibid.

238 Young, K. *What to say (and not to say) to someone who's depressed*. Retrieved on 6 May 2020 from https://www.heysigmund.com/what-to-say-to-someone-who-is-depressed/.

239 Psych Central (2019). *Best things to say to someone who's depressed*. Retrieved on 6 May 2020 from https://psychcentral.com/lib/best-things-to-say-to-someone-whos-depressed/.

240 Thomas, F. (2020). *10 things to say to someone with depression*. Retrieved on 6 May 2020 from https://www.headstogether.org.uk/10-things-to-say-to-someone-with-depression/.

241 Young, K. *What to say (and not to say) to someone who's depressed*. Retrieved on 6 May 2020 from https://www.heysigmund.com/what-to-say-to-someone-who-is-depressed/.

242 Thomas, F. (2020). *10 things to say to someone with depression.* Retrieved on 6 May 2020 from https://www.headstogether.org.uk/10-things-to-say-to-someone-with-depression/.

243 Ibid.

244 American Psychiatric Association (2013). *Diagnostic and Statistical Manual of Mental Disorders,* Fifth Edition, American Psychiatric Publishing, Washington, D.C. p. 161.

245 Hurley, K. (2018). *Helping someone with depression: What people want to hear (and what they don't).* Retrieved on 6 May 2020 from https://www.psycom.net/5-phrases-to-help-someone-with-depression.

246 Ibid.

247 Find Your Words (2020). *What to say to someone who's depressed.* Retrieved on 6 May 2020 from https://findyourwords.org/support-someone-with-depression/what-to-say-to-someone/.

248 Schimelpfening, N. (2020). *The worst things to say to someone who is depressed.* Retrieved on 6 May 2020 from https://www.verywellmind.com/worst-things-to-say-to-someone-who-is-depressed-1066982.

249 Kelly, M.A., Morse, J.Q., Stover, A. et al. (2011). Describing depression: Congruence between patient experiences and clinical assessments. *British Journal of Clinical Psychology,* vol. 50, no. 1, pp. 46-66. doi:10.1348/014466510X493926.

250 Schimelpfening, N. (2020). *The worst things to say to someone who is depressed.* Retrieved on 6 May 2020 from https://www.verywellmind.com/worst-things-to-say-to-someone-who-is-depressed-1066982.

251 Beyond Blue Ltd. *What not to say to someone with depression.* Retrieved on 6 May 2020 from https://www.beyondblue.org.au/personal-best/pillar/supporting-others/what-not-to-say-to-someone-with-depression.

252 Thomas, F. (2020). *10 things to say to someone with depression.* Retrieved on 6 May 2020 from https://www.headstogether.org.uk/10-things-to-say-to-someone-with-depression/.

253 Ibid.

254 Young, K. *What to say (and not to say) to someone who's depressed.* Retrieved on 6 May 2020 from https://www.heysigmund.com/what-to-say-to-someone-who-is-depressed/.

255 Beyond Blue Ltd. *What not to say to someone with depression.* Retrieved on 6 May 2020 from https://www.beyondblue.org.au/personal-

best/pillar/supporting-others/what-not-to-say-to-someone-with-depression.
256 Ibid.
257 Young, K. *What to say (and not to say) to someone who's depressed*. Retrieved on 6 May 2020 from https://www.heysigmund.com/what-to-say-to-someone-who-is-depressed/.
258 Schimelpfening, N. (2020). *The worst things to say to someone who is depressed*. Retrieved on 6 May 2020 from https://www.verywellmind.com/worst-things-to-say-to-someone-who-is-depressed-1066982.
259 Lépine, J.P. and Briley, M. (2011). The increasing burden of depression. Neuropsychiatr Dis Treat, vol. 7 (Suppl 1), pp. 3-7. doi:10.2147/NDT.S19617.
260 Schimelpfening, N. (2020). The worst things to say to someone who is depressed. Retrieved on 6 May 2020 from https://www.verywellmind.com/worst-things-to-say-to-someone-who-is-depressed-1066982.
261 Gotlib, I. and Hammen, C. (2002). *Handbook of depression*. New York: Guilford Press; *Preventing Suicide*, Centers for Disease Control and Prevention, reviewed on 5 September 2019; *10 leading causes of death and injury*, Centers for Disease Control and Prevention. Updated 10 April 2019.
262 Smith, K. PhD. (2019). *Suicide warning signs*. Retrieved on 13 May 2020 from https://www.psycom.net/suicide-warning-signs.
263 Ibid.
264 *Preventing suicide*, Centers for Disease Control and Prevention, Reviewed 5 September 2019; *10 leading causes of death and injury*, Centers for Disease Control and Prevention. Updated 10 April 2019.
265 Ferrari, A.J. et al. (2014). The burden attributable to mental and substance use disorders as risk factors for suicide: Findings from the Global Burden of Disease Study 2010. *PLoS ONE*, vol. 9, no. 4, p. e91936. https://doi.org/10.1371/journal.pone.0091936.
266 Gotlib, I. and Hammen, C. (2002). *Handbook of depression*. New York: Guilford Press; CDC (2020). *Preventing suicide*. Centers for Disease Control and Prevention. Updated 21 April 2020. Retrieved on 11 May 2020 from https://www.cdc.gov/violenceprevention/suicide/fastfact.html; CDC (2020). 10 Leading Causes of Death and Injury, Centers for Disease Control and Prevention. Updated 30 March 2020. Retrieved on 11 May 2020 from https://www.cdc.gov/injury/wisqars/LeadingCauses.html.

267 Ritchie, H. and Roser, M. (2020). Mental health. *Published online at OurWorldInData.org.* Retrieved on 16 April 2020 from https://ourworldindata.org/mental-health [online resource].

268 Ibid.

269 Australian Institute of Professional Counsellors (2015*). Suicide: Warning signs and prevention tips.* Retrieved on 8 May 2020 from https://www.aipc.net.au/articles/suicide-warning-signs-and-prevention-tips/.

270 Suicide Prevention Resource Center. *A comprehensive approach to suicide prevention.* Education Development Centre Inc. Retrieved on 13 May 2020 from https://www.sprc.org/effective-prevention/comprehensive-approach.

271 For example, see Smith, K. PhD. (2019). *Suicide warning signs.* Retrieved on 13 May 2020 from https://www.psycom.net/suicide-warning-signs; American Foundation of Suicide Prevention, *Risk factors and warning signs.* Retrieved on 13 May 2020 from https://afsp.org/risk-factors-and-warning-signs.

272 Australian Institute of Professional Counsellors (2015). *Suicide: Warning signs and prevention tips*, 20 February. Retrieved on 8 May 2020 from https://www.aipc.net.au/articles/suicide-warning-signs-and-prevention-tips/; Smith, K. PhD. (2019). *Suicide warning signs*, 9 September 2019. Retrieved on 13 May 2020 from https://www.psycom.net/suicide-warning-signs; American Foundation of Suicide Prevention, *Risk factors and warning signs.* Retrieved on 13 May 2020 from https://afsp.org/risk-factors-and-warning-signs.

273 Schimelpfening, N. (2020). *The worst things to say to someone who is depressed*, 25 March. Retrieved on 6 May 2020 from https://www.verywellmind.com/worst-things-to-say-to-someone-who-is-depressed-1066982.

274 American Foundation of Suicide Prevention, *Risk factors and warning signs.* Retrieved on 13 May 2020 from https://afsp.org/risk-factors-and-warning-signs.

275 Australian Institute of Professional Counsellors (2015). *Suicide: Warning signs and prevention tips*, 20 February. Retrieved on 8 May 2020 from https://www.aipc.net.au/articles/suicide-warning-signs-and-prevention-tips/; Smith, K. PhD. (2019). *Suicide warning signs*, 9 September. Retrieved on 13 May 2020 from https://www.psycom.net/suicide-warning-signs; American Foundation of Suicide Prevention,

Risk factors and warning signs. Retrieved on 13 May 2020 from https://afsp.org/risk-factors-and-warning-signs.

276 American Foundation of Suicide Prevention. *Risk factors and warning signs*. Retrieved on 13 May 2020 from https://afsp.org/risk-factors-and-warning-signs.

277 Saad, A.M., Gad, M.M. and Al-Husseini, M.J. et al. (2019). Suicidal death within a year of a cancer diagnosis: A population-based study. *Cancer*, vol. 125, no. 6, pp. 972-979. doi:10.1002/cncr.31876.

278 Ainsworth, M. (2011). *What can I do to help someone who may be suicidal?* Metanoia.org. Retrieved on 8 May 2020 from https://metanoia.org/suicide/whattodo.htm; Smith, M., Segal, J. and Robinson, L. (2012). *Suicide prevention: Spotting the signs and helping a suicidal person*. Helpguide.org. Retrieved on 8 May 2020 from https://www.helpguide.org/articles/suicide-prevention/suicide-prevention.htm.

279 For others see, for example, Florida Office of Drug Control. (2009). *Understanding & preventing suicide: A customizable Powerpoint training*. Florida Office of Drug Control. Statewide Office of Suicide Prevention and Suicide Prevention Coordinating Council. Retrieved on 8 May 2020 from http://www.helppromotehope.com/documents/Understanding&PreventingSuicide.ppt cited by Australian Institute of Professional Counsellors (2015). *Suicide: Warning signs and prevention tips*, 20 February. Retrieved on 8 May 2020 from https://www.aipc.net.au/articles/suicide-warning-signs-and-prevention-tips/.

280 Australian Institute of Professional Counsellors (2015). *Suicide: Warning signs and prevention tips,* 20 February. Retrieved on 8 May 2020 from https://www.aipc.net.au/articles/suicide-warning-signs-and-prevention-tips/.

281 Ainsworth, M. (2011). *What can I do to help someone who may be suicidal?* Metanoia.org. Retrieved on 8 May 2020 from https://metanoia.org/suicide/whattodo.htm; Smith, M., Segal, J. and Robinson, L. (2012). *Suicide prevention: Spotting the signs and helping a suicidal person.* Helpguide.org. Retrieved on 8 May 2020 from https://www.helpguide.org/articles/suicide-prevention/suicide-prevention.htm; Australian Institute of Professional Counsellors (2015). *Suicide: Warning signs and prevention tips*, 20 February. Retrieved on 8 May 2020 from https://www.aipc.net.au/articles/suicide-warning-signs-and-prevention-tips/; Smith, K. PhD. (2019). *Suicide warning signs*, 9 September. Retrieved on 13 May 2020 from https://www.psycom.net/suicide-warning-signs; American Foundation of Suicide Prevention, *Risk factors and warning*

signs. Retrieved on 13 May 2020 from https://afsp.org/risk-factors-and-warning-signs.

282 Ainsworth, M. (2011). *What can I do to help someone who may be suicidal?* Metanoia.org. Retrieved on 8 May 2020 from https://metanoia.org/suicide/whattodo.htm; Smith, M., Segal, J. and Robinson, L. (2012). *Suicide prevention: Spotting the signs and helping a suicidal person*. Helpguide.org. Retrieved on 8 May 2020 from https://www.helpguide.org/articles/suicide-prevention/suicide-prevention.htm; Australian Institute of Professional Counsellors (2015). *Suicide: Warning signs and prevention tips*, 20 February. Retrieved on 8 May 2020 from https://www.aipc.net.au/articles/suicide-warning-signs-and-prevention-tips/; Smith, K. PhD. (2019). *Suicide warning signs*, 9 September. Retrieved on 13 May 2020 from https://www.psycom.net/suicide-warning-signs; American Foundation of Suicide Prevention, *Risk factors and warning signs*. Retrieved on 13 May 2020 from https://afsp.org/risk-factors-and-warning-signs.

283 American Foundation of Suicide Prevention, *Risk factors and warning signs*. Retrieved on 13 May 2020 from https://afsp.org/risk-factors-and-warning-signs.

284 Australian Institute of Professional Counsellors (2015). *Suicide: Warning signs and prevention tips*, 20 February. Retrieved on 8 May 2020 from https://www.aipc.net.au/articles/suicide-warning-signs-and-prevention-tips/.

285 Schimelpfening, N. (2020). *The worst things to say to someone who is depressed,* 25 March. Retrieved on 6 May 2020 from https://www.verywellmind.com/worst-things-to-say-to-someone-who-is-depressed-1066982.

286 Australian Institute of Professional Counsellors (2015). *Suicide: Warning signs and prevention tips*, 20 February. Retrieved on 8 May 2020 from https://www.aipc.net.au/articles/suicide-warning-signs-and-prevention-tips/; Schimelpfening, N. (2020). *The worst things to say to someone who is depressed*, 25 March. Retrieved on 6 May 2020 from https://www.verywellmind.com/worst-things-to-say-to-someone-who-is-depressed-1066982.

287 Schimelpfening, N. (2020). *The worst things to say to someone who is depressed,* 25 March. Retrieved on 6 May 2020 from https://www.verywellmind.com/worst-things-to-say-to-someone-who-is-depressed-1066982.

288 Australian Institute of Professional Counsellors (2015). *Suicide: Warning signs and prevention tips*, 20 February. Retrieved on 8 May 2020 from https://www.aipc.net.au/articles/suicide-warning-signs-and-prevention-tips/.

289 Ibid.

290 Once the person is out of immediate danger, work with them to develop a safety plan. According to the Australian Institute of Professional Counsellors this is 'a set of steps that they commit to following if they have another suicidal crisis. Jointly list triggers that are more likely to bring on a crisis for the person; these could include anniversaries of losses, stress from relationships, employment issues, and abuse of alcohol or drugs. Make sure to list contact numbers of all relevant health professionals: doctors, psychiatrists, counsellors, etc. Put down the names of family members and friends who have agreed to help out in an emergency.' Australian Institute of Professional Counsellors (2015). *Suicide: Warning signs and prevention tips,* 20 February. Retrieved on 8 May 2020 from https://www.aipc.net.au/articles/suicide-warning-signs-and-prevention-tips/.

291 Beyond Blue Ltd, *Self-care for the supporter*. Undated. Retrieved on 8 May 2020 from https://www.beyondblue.org.au/the-facts/suicide-prevention/worried-about-someone-suicidal/self-care-for-the-supporter.

About the Author

ROBERT NICHOLLS is a freelance writer. This is his first book. His blog, robertnicholls.online, is focused on mental health (depression and anxiety), self-help, personal development, business, governance, leadership, life, society and culture. Nicholls lives on the Gold Coast in Queensland, Australia.

www.ingramcontent.com/pod-product-compliance
Lightning Source LLC
Chambersburg PA
CBHW070257010526
44107CB00056B/2491